Doctor After Arnhem

Witness to the Fall of the Third Reich

DOCTOR AFTER ARNHEM

WITNESS TO THE FALL OF
THE THIRD REICH

Stuart Mawson

SPELLMOUNT

British Library Cataloguing in Publication Data:
A catalogue record for this book is available
from the British Library

ISBN 1-86227-344-8

Published in the UK in 2006
by
Spellmount Limited
The Mill, Brimscombe Port
Stroud, Gloucestershire, GL5 2QG
Staplehurst
Kent TN12 0BJ

Tel: 01453 883300
Fax: 01453 883233
E-mail: enquiries@spellmount.com
Website: www.spellmount.com

1 3 5 7 9 8 6 4 2

Printed in Great Britain by
Oaklands Book Services
Stonehouse, Gloucestershire GL10 3RQ

Contents

	Preface	vii
I	Apeldoorn	1
II	Hospital Train	13
III	Falingbostel (9 October – 16 November 1944)	27
IV	Journey (16 – 20 November, 1944)	57
V	Naunhof 20 November – 14 December)	73
VI	Leipzig (14 December, 1944 – 6 March 1945)	91
VII	Naunhof (6 March – 21 April, 1945)	145

"Facilis descencus Averno:
Nocte atque dies patet atri ianua Ditis;
Sed revocare gradum superasque evadere ad auras,
Hoc opus, hic labor est."
                                        Virgil.

The way down to Hell is easy:
Night and day the jaws of darkness lie open;
But to arrest your step and climb back to the light of day,
This must be the endeavour, this the task.

Preface

On Monday 18 September 1944 I was dropped into the Battle of Arnhem as Regimental Medical Officer to the 11th Parachute Battalion, commanded by then Lieutenant Colonel, later General Sir George Lea. We had all been eager to go and thought it was going to be a walk-over, a piece of cake. But it blew up in our faces.

At the briefings the 1st Airborne Division was given to expect only minor opposition from the enemy, and to have to hold the bridge and the town not longer than forty-eight hours.

In the event this intelligence proved faulty. II SS Panzer Corps had been moved from Belgium and was refitting in bivouac areas just north of the town, with two divisions, the 9th and 10th within easy striking distance. They struck, and we found ourselves locked in a ferocious combat that lasted from the 17th, when the first airborne soldiers landed, until the night of the 25th/26th when the last man out crossed the river to the south bank.

My battalion was cut up on the 19th and I became separated from its chain of command, eventually joining up with the 181 Airlanding (Gliderborne) Field Ambulance, commanded by Lieutenant Colonel A.T. Marrable, which had established itself as a Dressing Station in the Hotel Schoonoord at Oosterbeek. There we doctors exerted ourselves to cope with an ever-deteriorating situation, being subjected to daily bombardments due to our position on a cross-road of tactical importance in close proximity to Divisional Headquarters. The building, crammed with wounded, gradually fell apart. Water, electricity and sewage services failed early on, medical and food supplies later. But we kept going, buoyed up by hope of relief by the main liberation army advancing from the south, until the contraction of ground held by our troops left us in the hands of the enemy.

I have given an account of my experiences in this phase of my medical life in *Arnhem Doctor*. What now follows is the sequel.

I

Apeldoorn

So Operation Market, the Arnhem end of Market Garden, was all but over, and we had bought it. The German Lieutenant Medical Officer, beside whom I was sitting in the back of a car outside the shambles of the Hotel Schoonoord at Oosterbeek on the evening of Sunday 24 September 1944, said to me, 'now for you the war is finished. Would you like a cigarette?' He spoke in French. My ability with this language, although very limited, had been my undoing. On the strength of previous parleys he had selected me to accompany him to an unknown destination. He had said there were British wounded who were becoming uncooperative, because he could not make them understand his treatment was for their own good, and he thought I would be able to help him to put himself across.

More than six hundred wounded had already been evacuated by the Germans from the captured Schoonoord which had, with some adjacent buildings, served as the main Royal Army Dressing Station for the grim stand of the airborne forces on the Oosterbeek bridgehead; an ever-contracting perimeter on the north bank of the Neder Rhine, referred to by the Germans as the 'Cauldron'. I had been there for the best part of a week, and had been hopeful of slipping away with my sergeant and batman and rejoining the remnants of my battalion, the 11th, now under Major Richard Lonsdale, down by the river during the coming night

1

– anything to avoid going permanently into the bag. But now I was undone and in a state of total abjection.

My recollection of what happened during the night in question, 24th/25th September, is extremely hazy. I was utterly weary, out on my feet from lack of sleep and food, suffering badly, I would have said of a similar case in civvy street, from severe nervous exhaustion. I was aware of the car drawing up in front of some building or other, and of being shown into a kind of small, candle-lit office where there was a straw-stuffed mattress on the floor, and being given a bowl of soup. After that I must have hit the mattress and gone straight off.

I was shaken awake by a German lance corporal, who indicated by signs that he wished me to tidy myself up, and then proceeded to unshutter the window. By the pale light that was thus afforded entry I read my watch; 0600 hours.On previous mornings, at this hour precisely, the Germans had always started to stonk us with mortars. I was half-way across the room, in a conditioned reflex, to slam the shutters, before I remembered. I was a prisoner of the Reich, well and truly in it. Outside everything was quiet and peaceful. The fighting had finished. I complied with the lance corporal's instructions. Presently the lieutenant appeared, looking about as bleary-eyed as I felt.

'Bonjour mon capitaine ... you have passed a good night?'

We exchanged a few pleasantries and then, changing his tone of voice, he said, 'circumstances have changed. You will be rejoining your col-leagues. I am putting you on an ambulance that is going to Oosterbeek to continue the evacuation. You will stay on it'.

'And then?'

'You will be taken to the prisoner of war hospital at Apeldoorn. Come.'

I wanted to remonstrate, to vent my feelings on him for having need-lessly wasted my one best opportunity of getting back across the river, but resignedly I nodded my assent and picked up my belongings. I had better get used to the idea that I was now entirely at the beck and call of my captors. In the German Army orders were certainly orders and they had me. My morale was at a very low ebb, and I even failed to resent being ordered about by one junior in rank to myself. I followed him meekly outside. A convoy of vehicles, a motley assembly of lorries, cars and a few proper ambulances, was parked in the rubble-littered street. The Lieutenant ushered me into the back of the leading one, a tail-drop lorry. I glanced quickly around. No way out of that with the eyes of the driver following boring into it.

'Au revoir capitaine.'

'Au revoir.'

I moved into the darker depths of the lorry, which had a backless metal bench down each side with space on the floor for stretchers, and sat in a corner. I still felt very tired and depressed, and closed my eyes as it bumped and jolted over the torn-up pavé. The Germans had not seen fit to give me any breakfast, and I doubted whether there would be anything to eat at the dressing station. But I was beyond caring. I seemed to have no will of my own left any more and was in a mood of black despair, until the lorry pulled up outside the Schoonoord and the sound of British voices jerked me out of it.

The Schoonoord had once been a thriving hotel–restaurant with spotlessly clean windows. Now not a single pane of glass was left, and the frames had mostly been boarded up with pieces of wood salvaged from the upper story and roof, which had been pounded to a collapse. The walls were pock-marked with hits from mortar and shell fragments and in places there were gaping holes where shots from German 88mm guns had penetrated the building.

The area abounded in trees dressed in their early autumn foliage, now all more or less shredded and stripped, while the cross-road, on which the hotel stood, was a junk-yard of smashed vehicles, disabled guns, discarded shell-cases and human remains, the last in the process of being collected for burial by men of both nationalities with red-cross armbands. At the hotel entrance, or what remained of it, were gathered a dirty crowd of airborne wounded and Royal Army Medical Corps personnel. I made to get out of the lorry but was waved back by the driver who had left his seat to supervise the loading. I looked for my sergeant and batman among the crowd, but could not see them. Had they managed to get away?

Soon I was involved in helping men into the lorry and in the automatic work of adjusting bandages and giving encouragement. They all seemed in a cheerful frame of mind, in fact able to affect me more than I them. Optimism is as catching as its opposite, and they were unquenchably optimistic. We were, after all, still in Arnhem, and the sound of the main engagement taking place south of the river as the Guards Armoured Division strove to reach us was clearly audible. They made me realise I had been passing through a mental process of sheer defeatism; passing through because once I saw it for what it was I felt ashamed, and resolved thereupon to kick it. The Allies had won the war, I knew that for the sober truth, and it was but a question of time. 'You must rally', I told myself. 'No matter what befalls never let the enemy see you dispirited,'

The convoy set off along the main road to Arnhem, stopping every now and again to manoeuvre past a fallen lamp-post or tree, or to disentangle a vehicle from trailing telephone wires. We were proceeding along the main axis of the abortive divisional advance towards the centre of the town, and everywhere there was evidence of the relentless battle of attrition waged between the crack units of the respective armies. Houses on either side of the road all bore scars, some had been pulverised almost to ground level, others were merely chipped and pitted. Strewn around was the wreckage of war, discarded equipment, burnt overturned cars, here and there an abandoned tank, rubble, shell-holes, fires still smouldering, a few coloured supply parachutes draped forlornly on fractured trees, and the dead of both sides lying desolately in the gutters and gardens where they had fallen. Soon we began to pass groups of Dutch civilians, whole families, each with an enormous bundle of belongings on their backs, trudging weariliy along the road. I was now standing with others at the open back-end of the canvas-topped truck and as we went by we gave them the Churchill 'V' sign, and tried with smiles and greetings to make them understand they were not to lose heart. Some smiled back in return, others shook their fists at us and yet others wept openly. This was one of our saddest moments. We had arrived as liberators and were leaving as prisoners. Arnhem had suffered enormous damage and, from the Dutch point of view, all to no purpose, for the Germans were still there; and the Dutch knew and we knew their lot would now be a great deal worse instead of better. We shared their disappointment and understood their despair. The marvel was that any of them were still defiant and smiling.

The German driver of our truck was alone in front and gave us scant attention. We were unguarded and unarmed, and presumably considered harmless. It would have been a simple matter for any of the able-bodied, including myself, to have dropped over the tailgate for we were proceeding at a snail's pace. But the area was stiff with Germans, we were in view of the driver following and would not have stood a chance. We had, moreover, been told that if we so much as attempted to leave the truck we should be shot. Yet there had already begun the process of discussion and calculation indicative of an offensive spirit, relating to escape, that kept the senses sharpened for an eye to the main chance.

Eventually, after having negotiated the centre and left behind all evidence of fighting, we moved out of Arnhem and drove northwards down a straight tree-lined road into open country. There were again a lot of Dutch civilians trundling themselves and their possessions away from the stricken town. Old ladies were being pushed along in wheel-barrows by older men, younger men, still boys really, were carrying children on their shoulders, young girls were riding bicycles. If anyone were so lucky

4

as to possess a horse and cart the poor beast was almost submerged by the load of humanity and luggage perched, however precariously, on top.

The further we got away from Arnhem the more friendly we found the people – presumably they had not suffered so much from our invasion – and our 'V' signs were returned enthusiastically. If, as happened quite frequently, there were columns of Germans on the road, the Dutch would disguise their 'V' sign, combining it with such innocent gestures as blowing their noses or scratching their heads. This pantomime unexpectedly engendered a jocund atmosphere, almost a carnival spirit, amongst what, in reality, was a sad procession of refugees and a convoy of battered prisoners of war. We had been going for about half an hour, in fits and starts because of the crowds, along the same road, when some Allied fighters, Typhoons, approached from the south. Their appearence caused pandemonium. All the Dutch ran helter-skelter for the fields and abruptly threw themselves on the ground, abandoning their belongings, as though playing some strange adult game of ring-a-roses. The convoy rocked to a stop, and the drivers leaped from their cabins and hurled themselves into a ditch by the roadside. Ours, having concealed himself to his satisfaction, poked his head up sufficiently to keep us under observation and pointed his rifle uncompromisingly in our direction. The fighters dived and came sailing in toward us, while we waved and cheered, in the possibly misplaced confidence that the large red crosses painted on the tops of the vehicles would guarantee immunity from attack. Apparently they had targets other than the odd German column, for having looked us over they wheeled away to the east, and the drivers climbed sheepishly out of the ditch, discomforted and, we hoped, annoyed by our broad smiles.

We drove on and reached a country town which I took to be Apeldoorn, the site of Queen Wilhelmina of the Netherlands country residence. None of us knew it or had been there before but we sensed we had reached our destination. Soon we arrived at some guarded and wired gates giving entry to a large fenced-in area. After an exchange of formalities between the sentries and driver we passed through, following a drive until we drew up outside a complex of modern barrack buildings.

The Caserne Wilhelm III, for so it proved to be, was arranged in several blocks. The convoy drew up at the central one and we began to disembark. Captain Theo Redman of the 133 Parachute Field Ambulance advanced to meet us. I knew him only slightly but enough to grip his proferred hand with a 'Hello Redman. Damn good to see you'. He flinched a little and smiled wrily, gingerly applying his left hand to his right upper-arm. 'You're OK I hope', I said anxiously.

'Oh sure. Just a little flesh wound. Bullet on the bloody DZ. Ran into a reception committee of Dutch SS troops. Been in the bag ever since. And you?'

'Got separated from the battalion a week ago and wandered around like a lost soul until I hooked onto Marrable's outfit at Oosterbeek'.

'You mean at the Schoornoord?'

'Yes. That was a nice place once.'

'We've got a few hundred of the chaps from there here already.' I nodded towards the convoy. 'All these are from there, and more to come.'

'In that case,' he said, 'you'd better come right in and give me a hand. I'm putting together nominal rolls and trying to sort the wounded into proper categories of who needs what in the way of treatment.'

We went inside where there was a table covered with papers, and an RAMC clerk sitting at work. The Reception, or so the entrance hall was placarded, was thronged like the concourse of an airport during a strike. Men squatted, lounged or lay on stretchers with their personal belongings in uncomfortable, crowded groups waiting to be called to their allotted places. Redman and I went round examining the casualty cards tied to each, which gave details of the wounds and the treatment so far received, and noted what we thought would next be required, and where in the building he should go.

The Germans had allotted us three barrack blocks, each block a three storey compact with a holding capacity of some three hundred and fifty wounded, provided some use was made of double bunks. Considering the late stage of the war facilities were very good, with central heating, good washrooms, bath-houses and showers, and modern sanitation. Redman, together with Lieutenant Colonel Herford, who had managed to cross the river from the south as an envoy of 30 Corps to negotiate medical aid for the beleaguered Oosterbeek perimeter, only to be detained by the Germans, had both worked non-stop since yesterday.

They each spoke German and had done much to smooth the way and lay the foundation of a satisfactory working relation between ourselves and our captors. All day we dealt with a constant inflow of wounded accompanied, thankfully, by a large proportion of all the doctors and RAMC personnel who had descended from the skies. Finally, in the early evening the last lorry-load arrived bearing the senior medical officer of the division (ADMS), Colonel G M Warrack with his HQ staff, and Lieutenant Colonel A T Marrable with his, and right glad we were to see them. Right glad too was I, after greetings had been exchanged, to find the next item on the agenda was to be an evening meal. I had become used to eating little or nothing in the concluding stages of the battle and now the mention of food made me realise how ravenous I was. The issue of two slices of German blackbread and lard, with a bowl of soup seemed princely at that moment, but needless to say that reaction did not last long, as each meal subsequently turned out to be a variation on the same theme. The lard was disgusting. To get it down meant covering it liberally with salt. Not to get it down was unthinkable as the pangs of hunger were never properly assuaged. But that first meal was a merry one. When we realised how lucky so many of us doctors had been in surviving at all and in finding ourselves together, the tremendous collective spirit of the airborne division took hold of us, and our morale went sky high. Major Pip Smith, a surgeon with the 16th Parachute Field Ambulance and known to me from medical school days, was the first to broach the subject that became uppermost, certainly in my mind, once the hilarity had quietened down. 'What's the security like?' We all looked at Redman.

'Tell us,' I prompted, 'you've been here longer than any of us. What are the chances of a break?'

Redman looked thoughtful. 'I haven't had time yet to find out very much. But I do know the place is surrounded by a ten-foot high steel fence reinforced with concertina barbed wire. You've seen the guard house at the gate. Sentries are constantly on patrol round the blocks and I believe they bring in Alsatian dogs at night.'

We must have looked glum.

'It's early days yet,' he went on, 'once we're properly organised we'll have every inch of the place mapped out. We'll find the loopholes and what we can't find we'll make. The ADMS will be briefing officers in the morning. I suggest those who haven't been told off for night duty get some kip as soon as possible, There's going to be a hell of a lot to do.'

During the night increasing medical order was caused to grow out of the chaos of wounded and RAMC personnel dumped unceremoniously from a diversity of army units into the unprepared barracks. From having functioned in self-contained parcels, further fragmented by the German onslaught, all had now to be welded into the cohesive unity of a military hospital. When I came down for the briefing after a profound sleep on a straw mattress in a wooden bunk, the machinery already had a polished and well-oiled look. Not many of the senior doctors could have had much rest for, as I was about to learn, the organisational framework had been hammered out, with jobs allocated and use of space apportioned in detail;'Reception', 'Theatres', 'Resuscitation', 'Wards', 'Officers Mess', 'Sergeants Mess', 'Other Ranks' Mess', all had been sorted out and sign-posted.

The barracks had been set aside by the Germans for the sole use of the airborne medical services to be run by ourselves. They had their own problems in terms of some two and a half thousand wounded requiring accommodation in other hospitals in the area with their own medical services stretched to the limit. Colonel Warrack outlined the situation which, after the grim difficulties met with in the battle, seemed distinctly encouraging. The British wounded were estimated at two thousand or so, more than could be accommodated at one time in the barracks, but the Germans aimed to carry out a steady evacuation of our wounded to Germany, and to bring in outliers to fill their places until all the British wounded were here. Ultimately, as they became fit enough to travel they would be sent to the Reich in batches by rail. On our side we had perhaps twenty qualified doctors, a few dentists and padres and about four hundred RAMC personnel. Given the priority that everything done must in the first instance be for the benefit of the wounded, our next main priority would be to hinder the German plans for evacuation to the Reich by every possible and conceivable means, we could see ahead for a few weeks at least. The Liberation Army was still only a few miles south of Arnhem, and comfortingly audible. The barracks would, from now on, be referred to as the Airborne Military Hospital, organised along conventional military lines with an HQ, Administrative Wing, Medical Wing and Registrar. The Medical Wing, to be commanded by Lieutenant Colonel W C Alford (OC 133 Parachute Field Ambulance), would be divided into three blocks, A, B and C, and used to full capacity, each with its own theatre and treatment rooms. I was assigned to Block C with sixty patients to look after, which included most of the officer patients.

The wounded had straw-stuffed mattresses under them, which they declared felt like the best interior-sprung after having lain for days on blood-soaked stretchers, but they were in short supply, as were blankets, at first. Scores of severely wounded continued to arrive and it took another two days before something like proper order prevailed. The Germans were co-operative and seemed anxious to do what they could to ease the shortages. More mattresses and blankets appeared to match the hospital's capacity and once saturation level was reached no more wounded were brought in. The situation then became stabilised, all were comfortably berthed and hospital routine got into full swing. Food at this stage, however, remained very short, and had an adverse effect both on the recuperative powers of the wounded and the doctors' capacity for work. We had to be on our legs, working hard the whole time, and the end of the day found us exhausted and bad tempered. It required a constant mental effort to keep going. I found myself having to fight a tendency to want to put off the examination of wounds, the changing of dressings and the writing up of case records. These inner fights themselves added to fatigue, while to us, in those days, the absence of cigarettes was about the last straw calculated to break the camel's back. Whatever might be thought about them medically now, they had a soothing, and appetite-blunting effect that was sorely missed.

In the mess, in the evenings, after wolfing our meagre rations, the time was passed playing cards, poker or cribbage for most, bridge for an esoteric few, and in discussing the estimated progress of the second army or the opportunities for escape. Redman informed us that the steel railings and concertina barbed wire surround was deficient in a portion of the eastern end of the perimeter, and replaced by a single-strand thickness barbed wire fence. He thought this was a potential weakness that might be exploited, although it overlooked open fields with no cover and was certain to be patrolled by guards. Some of the earlier admitted walking-wounded, about five hundred, had already been evacuated to Germany in cattle trucks, and their departure gave an urgent impetus to those remaining to look to all possible means of avoiding the same one-way journey.

The hospital was at first guarded by elements of the SS, but after several days these were replaced by elderly gentlemen from the Wehrmacht, who became affectionately referred to as the Bismark Youth. Before the SS guards departed they instituted a thorough search for anything that might be construed as an aid to escape. We were locked into our rooms while half a dozen toughs picked over our belongings. They were not very successful. Escape kits were hidden, mine behind a radiator, and most of us retained at least a mini-map of northern Europe printed on a handkerchief, and a small compass. As soon as superficial wounds began to heal and men became fitter a steady trickle of escapes were achieved through the weak area in the security fence. The CO was at pains to make it clear that, while help would be given to those who wished to try their luck, there must be strict coordination of plans. No mass breakouts could be contemplated, escape requests must be made to himself or his deputy, and medical officers must stay put as long as there were wounded requiring attention. The question of escape for the doctors could only seriously be considered after the wounded had been evacuated to Germany. It was the prevention of this to which we must put our minds, striving to keep the hospital as full as possible as long as possible in the firm faith that the Second Army had the potential to relieve us and would do so shortly. Anything might happen. The Sixth Airborne Division was again available after the Normandy landings and might be used to secure another bridgehead. The German panzer units that had so unexpectedly put in an appearance at Arnhem and swung the battle against the First Airborne Division might be neutralised by the Allied air forces while Horrock's Armour forced a passage over the bridge which, as far as we knew, was still intact. All this we now know was wishful thinking, but at the time it kept us going.

At the beginning of the second week three things of importance happened to us. The first was an improvement in the quantity and, to some extent, quality, of the food. We went to bed less hungry although by no means satisfied. The second was a consignment of cigarettes. These had been gradually trickling in through the good offices of the Dutch Red Cross and now suddenly became quite plentiful; by carefully rationing oneself to four or five a day a reserve could be built up against future shortages. The third was of far more moment. The Germans managed, despite constant attacks from the Allied airforces and ground sabotage by the Dutch, to get two hospital trains into the station at Apeldoorn. One of these was a properly equipped hospital train with bunks, sanitary facilities and, the mark of real authenticity, a staff of female nurses. The other, so-called by the Germans, was nothing of the kind, a mere string of cattle trucks painted with red crosses intended for the transport of lightly or walking wounded. Hardly had the news of these trains reached us, as indeed all outside news reached us, through the Dutch Underground and Red Cross rather than the Germans, who never gave advance notice of their intentions, gave orders for two hundred and fifty walking wounded to be made ready to leave in the cattle-truck train in two hours, accompanied by three doctors. Colonel Warrack fought for time, while we all bit our nails waiting for his decision as to which of us would be the three to go. He argued forcibly with the Germans that cattle trucks were inadequate for the transport of wounded. It was known that red crosses on cattle trucks were suspect as possible cover for transport of war material and would be liable to air attack. A train of passenger-sized coaches so marked was another matter. The Senior German Medical Officer was sympathetic, apologetic, but adamant. Owing to the circumstances of the war proper hospital trains were in short supply. Their own wounded had to travel in such trucks. The floors would be covered by ample layers of straw, there would be only twenty men to each and frequent stops would be made for refreshments and the needs of nature.

Selecting the wounded for this train was an unwelcome task. While the Germans stood at our elbows urging us on to pick the men as quickly as possible, we did our best to delay, playing the CO's recommended game of 'daft laddie'; holding long discussions on each case, re-examining wounds and mislaying nominal rolls. If the German order had been carried out to the letter the party would have moved off in full daylight.

In the event we gained, at least, enough time to ensure that when they reached the station it would be getting dark with greater opportunity for individual attempts at escape. The individuals chosen were duly paraded, searched and given each a blanket to take with him. As for the doctors, we waited unhappily for the CO to choose the unfortunates among us who would appear to be about to forfeit any chance of liberation by the Second Army. Eventually he chose a doctor from each brigade, Captain Keesey of the 1st Parachute (soon to be shot dead trying to escape), Captain Lawson of the 4th Parachute, and Captain Simmons of the Airlanding (Gliderborne). Captain Ridler, Dental Officer of the 16th Parachute Field Ambulance was also detailed. The news was brought to me by an RAMC sergeant. 'You're all right, sir. We'll be home for Christmas yet if the BLA stops bloody-well larking about and gets a move on in this direction.'

The CO and Colonel Herford were permitted to visit the train that evening and what they had to report back made us all very angry. There were thirty men to a truck, not twenty as promised, no sanitary arrangements, inadequate rations, and the trucks were wired and locked once the wounded were inside. Moreover the red crosses on the roofs were far too small as effective deterrents to air attack. The CO let it be known he had protested strongly at the highest level but doubted much good would come of it. We seethed with indignation, especially those more junior doctors such as myself who had been personally involved in looking after the men. Next morning we felt better. News came in that the RAF had bombed a railway bridge east of Apeldoorn and the cattle-truck train was still in the station unable to be moved. We were also greeted by the sound of very heavy firing to the south, which we had very little difficulty in persuading ourselves was Allied artillery softening up German positions prior to forcing a crossing of the Neder Rhine. All through that day, Tuesday 3 October, we remained in a state of buoyant anticipation as the firing continued unabated, even when the news leaked through that the cattle-truck train had eventually left for Germany by a longer route, a single line track via the north of Holland. Those of us still at Apeldoorn felt we had every reason to remain hopeful. Ever since the break-out in Normandy we had become conditioned by events to expect a continual, rapid and successful advance by the Allied ground forces. The First Airborne Division had been briefed on numerous occasions to go into action, and then been stood down because the speed of advance on the ground had been such as to pre-empt the need for our intervention. We had actually cursed this speed for cutting out our chances for action. For, having stood by so often to go in and then been stood down, we had been living on our nerves, and had been eager to break the tension and get on with it. Now we were being held but fifteen miles north of the cutting edge of the British Liberation Army with the sound of guns like music in our ears.

No further orders came about the hospital train we knew was still in the station, and we did everything possible to persuade our captors none of our men were fit to move. Whenever a German doctor appeared in a ward the wounded piled on the agony. The British soldier is very resourceful and the *in extremis* acts put on for the Germans' benefit had us at times wondering about the true state of affairs. For two days we remained in a limbo of uncertainty as to our future, then the blow fell. The Germans signalled on the morning of the 6th that five hundred wounded were to be made ready in three hours to be put into ambulances destined for the hospital trains They also asked for seven doctors, a dentist, two padres and sixty medical orderlies to accompany the wounded. The decisions were made and my name was on the list.

Each one of us was the centre of his own private drama. While hope of liberation remained we were emotionally tied to it, experiencing lift and excitement when it ran high, bitterness and depression as it ran low. Now it looked as if it had run out. Today, unless a miracle occurred I would be on a train destined for Hitler's Reich. The knowledge, paradoxically, brought a perverse feeling of relief. My emotional yo-yo now lay inert at the bottom of its string. I would need to be rational and practical to cope with the unknown, depending not on others to rescue me from whatever predicament I found myself in, but on my own resourcefulness and calm appraisal of every new situation.

II

Hospital Train

The reports were correct. This was a proper hospital train. In every compartment set aside for the wounded beds were arranged in tiers of three along each side, with a heating stove at one end and sanitary facilities with running water at the other. There was a galley wagon, a carriage equipped as an operating theatre and separate quarters for officers and nursing sisters. It was commanded by a German doctor of the rank of major supported by two lieutenant doctors and two sisters. The whole British contingent, wounded and staff, was in charge of Lieutenant Colonel 'Bill' Alford, and we officers were assigned residential accommodation in the last coach but one, the last being a guard's van. Our coach was also occupied by an unsmiling and anxious-looking German orderly responsible for guarding us and fetching our rations from the galley. Theo Redman was among our party and, in his good German, lost no time in chatting up the guard. 'Franz', so we christened him, proved to be remarkably forthcoming, quickly admitting he hated his job, mainly on account of the Allied air forces, who made life for anyone working on the German railways an absolute misery. To emphasise the point he treated us to a wholly unexpected and astonishing solo representation of an air attack on the train, first spreading out his arms, weaving around the carriage and dt-dt-dting and boom-booming, like a schoolboy, then abandoning the role of pilot to become himself, throwing himself flat on the floor and covering the back of his head with his hands. That, he said, was how he spent most of his days and he was totally fed up. He as much as said he did not care what we did provided it did not get him into trouble. We could hardly contain ourselves, but sensing a potential ally kept our faces serious.

'Can this really be so?' I asked Theo, 'or is he off his rocker?'

'He's sane enough,' Theo replied, 'but he's really had it up to here.' Theo laid the back of his extended palm under his chin. 'He says the train we've all noticed alongside is not a gun transporter but a fully-manned flak train, and he's expecting trouble in the morning.'

'That means they're using the red crosses on our train as cover,' Bill Alford put in, 'that is quite contrary to the Geneva Convention and totally unacceptable. I must speak to the train commandant. Ask Franz to take me to him.'

Franz was all in favour and hurried the colonel up the platform. They returned in about half an hour.

'Warrack already knows about this,' Alford informed us, 'has taken it up with the senior German doctor in the area and is trying to get the flak train moved. All the German medicos seem to be on our side. They're very short of hospital trains and can see it isn't every pilot who'll refrain from going for the flak just because we're next to it. Dicey situation.' We all agreed.

After dark, while Franz was collecting our evening rations from the galley, we discussed the feasibility of escape. Alford took the view that the station was too heavily guarded to offer any real chance of success. There were look-outs on the flak train, soldiers patrolling the platform and guards on the exits. We should have to take it as it came and hope for opportunities to present themselves when and if the train got on the move. Besides, he was not sure how many officers he would be able to spare. While the train was full of our wounded they would need our care. We had the freedom to pass up and down the train to and from our allot-ted compartments. Alford had assigned us two each. Mine were at the far end. We prepared for bed wondering whether or not the train would pull out during the night. There was no engine attached as yet. Long might it remain so.

Next morning we were still there and Franz's prediction was realised. We had two early visitations from rocket-firing Typhoons. As they roared in the flak train opened up with everything it had got. The Typhoons, showing a superb disregard for the German ack-ack fire, sailed serenely over, ignoring us to concentrate on targets further east along the line. Soon we heard explosions and saw plumes of smoke which encouraged us no end. During the attack Franz, predictably, was lying on the floor of the compartment. We were too enthralled, and crowded onto the railed-in open platform at the end of the carriage to watch the show. Each carriage had one of these platforms at either end with steps by which entry was gained from station or track, and a metal bridge linking it with the adjacent one. RAMC orderlies were crammed on that next to ours, and we all waved and cheered as the aircraft passed over, while the perspiring German gunners shook their fists and, according to Theo, shouted obscenities and threats at us.

The attacks gave us a vicarious thrill, compensating for our own enforced inaction and presenting our imagination with the opportunity of envisaging the damage to the line we would dearly have loved to have been able to inflict ourselves in order to delay our departure. We were further cheered by a report that told of a strike by the Dutch railway workers and of active sabotage by the Dutch underground in an effort to isolate Apeldoorn station. We were full of admiration for Dutch tenacity in the face of vicious German reprisals. The Germans had, for example, on a recent occasion, we were told, ordered the whole male population out to dig defences on the banks of the river Ijssel, but out of several thousand potential workers only forty put in an appearance. So the Germans picked upon a score of Dutchmen, shot them and left their bodies at cross-roads and other prominent places in the town with placards round their necks reading 'This is the price of treason to Germany' or, simply, 'Traitor'. While at this juncture exuberant we were therefore cautious and correct in our response to German orders. They could turn nasty at any time. On a global scale we undoubtedly had them beaten, but here, parochially, the boot was on the other foot.

Later that same morning, somewhat to our surprise, the flak train moved out. There must have been very effective string-pulling in high places. The departure of this bone of contention was followed by a marked relaxation in the attitude of our captors. Franz actually managed a smile, and we spent a comparatively pleasant day, tending our patients and strolling up and down the platform in the warm autumn sunshine. Dutch children appeared, to gather as near as they dared to our train to goggle and stare. Some of the bolder ones lobbed apples at us which were juicy and delicious. If a German soldier came near they scattered in a flash, only to return in twos and threes as curiosity again got the better of alarm.

The food on the train was an improvement on that in the military hospital. We had margarine, a more liberal supply of bread and cold sausage, and thicker soup. Franz had exactly the same as ourselves so presumably we were, as the Geneva Convention required, on full German army rations. The black bread was the mainstay. Certainly it appeared so to Franz. He took his loaf and, holding it against his chest, lovingly cut off large chunks with his clasp knife, slicing towards himself in absorbed concentration. He then stuffed his mouth full and chewed contentedly with massive movements of his jaws, adding to his mouth, with the same clasp knife, bits of marge and sausage or whatever.

For us he used a bread knife to cut regulation slices thinly. This may have been a gentlemanly concession to our table habits, but I rather think derived from strict adherence to rationing and avoidance of waste.

As the afternoon wore on and, having finished the main medical work of the day, we took the opportunity for a short period of feet-up in our compartment prior to making the evening rounds. Suddenly there was a clatter and jolt. Alford swung himself off his bunk.

'That could be an engine. Being coupled on. Let's go and take a look.'

He led out. We filed after, but no more than two or three had descended the iron steps to the station platform when we were abruptly ushered back again by a German soldier brandishing a rifle. Franz, meanwhile, had clambered to his feet and now shouldered past us. He held a brief conversation with the other soldier, then indicated he wished us all to go back into the compartment Theo tackled him.

'It's an engine all right. Franz says no-one is allowed off the train from now on. We're to stay in here until we've been inspected and counted. All the symptoms and signs point to an impending move.'

Very shortly after this the Train Commandant appeared with a clerical orderly and held a roll-call. Satisfied we were all accounted for he made a short speech. Theo translated, 'free to move up and down the train to tend patients. Any attempt to leave the train or escape will be severely punished.' He did not, as a British officer might, finish by asking 'any questions', and none of us cared to venture an enquiry into what, exactly, he meant by punishment. The turn of events had us subdued. The commandant then consulted his list and read out the names of two of our junior doctors and the dentist. They were to leave the train immediately. No reason given. No word of their destination; just the order. Theo tried to press him for further information but he shook his head. Negative. Barking further instructions to Franz, he abruptly turned on his heel and departed. We were very uneasy. Our immediate future was again suddenly in question, both for those staying on the train, and those leaving whom Franz was now urging to collect their gear. Soon we were shaking their hands and he was marching them out. It felt like a parody of ten green bottles sitting on the wall. Now apart from the two padres we were a medical staff of six: the CO, two surgeons and three general duty medical officers, of which I was one and the most junior.

The sunny atmosphere of the earlier part of the day had quite dissipated after our friends had gone we sat gloomily in the compartment while Alford discussed with us the reallocation of duties to fill their gaps. We then dispersed up the train to familiarise ourselves with our new patients. This done, I returned to the compartment to find Franz had just returned and the others were gathered round him.

'Any news?'

'Franz has announced we shall soon be leaving for the Reich,' Theo volunteered.

'What part of the Reich?'

'He says it depends on the Luftwaffe – meaning ours.'

'The probability is it is true we shall soon be on our way' commented Alford, 'they will prefer to make the main movements at night when it is safer.'

The prophecy was correct. The train pulled out at about 1900 hours when it was almost dusk, but instead of moving in an easterly direction, towards Germany, our course seemed to be due north. We stood on the platform at the end of the compartment, watching the garden suburbs of Apeldoorn slip by. A thick ground mist was forming. Visibility was decreasing. The train was creaking along slowly. Franz was inside the coach, paying no attention to us, and the door was closed. We were alone, and staring, fascinated, at the side of the track. Suburbs gave way to open country. Bushes and other vegetation swam successively into view within a mere yard or so of the single line on which we were travelling. One of us, I think it was Redman, released the thought that surely had become uppermost in every mind.

'This is money for old rope. We may never get a better chance.' Everyone started to talk at once. 'get on the bottom step. Jump and roll.' 'A piece of cake.' 'A heaven sent gift.' 'What then?' 'Go south. Try to link with the second army.' 'No. Lie up and let them link with you.' 'No. Better to contact the Dutch underground let them handle it.'

'Hang on.' Alford's voice cut in, 'you're forgetting the patients and the fact that our staff is already depleted. The moment may be ripe but the choice is difficult. The question is where our duty lies as doctors. Here with the patients, five hundred of them, remember, or with the troops still fighting *if* we can manage to rejoin them. I've had to think hard about this and have decided I must stay. I am not giving any orders to anybody in particular but I would like some support. I would prefer not to lose more than one or, at the most, two of you. I will leave you to discuss it among yourselves.'

On the observation platform we talked and talked and thrashed it out while the precious minutes went by. The two padres went into a separate huddle and soon one of them announced,

17

'I'm going now. There is no need for two of us on this train, and what the CO said to you doesn't apply in quite the same way to us'. And he went inside to tell Alford and collect some gear. The two surgeons decided they must stay, which left we three general duty medical officers still grappling with the choice. I felt I would like to have a crack at it as did the other two, but our feelings for Alford determined an agreement it should only be one. But which? We thought of drawing lots, but eventually came to the conclusion that the chance should go to Redman. The argument prevailed that his knowledge of German would stand him in the better stead. It gave an additional dimension to his avoiding detection as he could read and understand all the notices in German plastered up everywhere, pass more easily as a Dutchman and, as they often had a better knowledge of German than English, especially in the rural northern area towards which we were moving, explain himself to them more easily. So we calculated.

At this point a corporal medical orderly from the adjoining coach came out onto his platform, a small haversack in hand. He looked at our group and singling out the senior of us, Major 'Pip' Smith, one of the surgeons, said he wanted to escape and had he permission?

'I'll have to ask the CO. Wait here.'

Smith entered the compartment soon to re-emerge to tell the corporal that the CO approved his attempt. Theo Redman moved first to one side of the platform then the other, thoughtfully studying the verges. Then he turned to the corporal.

'It will be best if you go at the same time as I. There's always a chance we may be observed, alone or together, as we go. If together, and we go one from each side, the Germans may hesitate at which one to shoot and give us the extra seconds we need to drop out of sight.'

Smith said, 'you'll be better off as a pair afterwards as well. Two pairs of eyes are better than one for lying up and keeping lookout, taking turnabout at sleep.'

'OK?' asked Redman.

'Fine', said the corporal.

'Right then. Come into our compartment with us. Drop your haversack on the nearest bunk and make as if you're reporting something to the colonel.'

'I've already told him about Theo.' Smith observed. 'He says we'll have to stage some kind of diversion to distract Franz's attention while you make the jump.'

We all sauntered back into the carriage. Alford beckoned us.

'Look casual, here's a pack of cards. Start a game of something. Light up and relax.'

18

We began a game of vingt-et-une while, between the calls of twist or bust, Alford heard Theo's plan for a simultaneous jump from each side of the platform.

'What about the padre?' he commented. The padre cut in.

'I'll take my chance alone and go first. If I get away with it you'll know your chances are good at that point.' He gave a wry smile, 'if not you will have saved yourselves some trouble.'

'OK,' said Alford, 'now what we will do is this.'

Alford and we three junior doctors went on playing cards. The two surgeons armed themselves with an army blanket, positioned themselves between Franz, who had his feet up reading at the other end of the compartment, and his line of vision with the door and ourselves, and staged an elaborate pantomime, pretending to fix the padre who was looking for a home-made overcoat from the blanket. This entailed holding it up against him athwart the compartment and, as soon as the show was under way, Theo quickly got a haversack of kit together and the platform party sidled out surreptitiously into the cold air. If Franz did notice our absence they were to try to make him understand we had gone off visiting patients.

Alford slid the door to and stood with his back to it. On his left Redman sat down on the steps, on his right the padre and corporal did likewise. I stood by Redman within touching distance of the other MO, who stood by the others. The intention was that after the padre had gone, and as soon as Redman jumped I would rap the other MO and he would give a 'Go' to the corporal. Alford would abort the jump in the event of a guard appearing, the padre coming to grief or any other unfavourable circumstances intervening.

It was now very much darker and the train was passing through wooded country, the single track running down a narrow lane cut between close ranks of fir trees. Speed had increased to about thirty miles an hour and the gap between train and trees was no more than a couple of yards.

'Don't like the look of it here,' said Redman quietly, 'too much risk of hitting a tree. I'll wait a bit.'

Then the train slowed to negotiate a left-hand bend. Suddenly we heard a stifled cry. 'This is it. Good-bye. Good luck followed by a muffled 'thrump' sound of a body hitting ground. I rushed to the right and peered backwards in time to see a kneeling figure with arm upraised, before the curve hid him from view. The padre had gone.

We waited tensely to see what might happen. Nothing. No alarm. The train just pottered on. The bend had been in his favour. Guards who might have been looking out on his, convex, side of the train would not easily have had him in view, those on the concave side not at all. It was a well chosen moment and he had got away – apparently without hitting a tree, and unhurt.

Heartened by this success we braced ourselves for the next move. Gradually the woods thinned out and the verges became grass and bushes, up to the very edge of the line.

'This looks more like it,' said Alford. 'Action stations.'

'Agreed', and Redman poised himself on the bottom step about three feet from the ground. I stood above him on the platform, right hand stretched out, holding my breath. Redman crouched as if ready to spring, looked left, right, then climbed back up the steps.

'Coming into a station. Quick, loll about. If anyone sees us they've got to think we're just taking the air.'

The train rattled over some points, stacks of timber loomed up by the side of the line, then a signal-box, then a station platform and buildings. The train had meanwhile rapidly slowed to a mere crawl.

Alford muttered under his breath, 'we can be in trouble if it stops. Keep going you bastard. The whisper was taken up. 'Keep going you bastard. Keep going.' I really thought at one moment it was about to stop but, to our unutterable relief, it did keep going and, what was more, the station was deserted. Our luck had held again.

Redman let out a 'phew' of compressed breath. 'I was on the very point of jumping. Damn good thing I saw what was coming.'

'Did you see a place name?' asked Alford.

'Afraid not. But it was small, too small for Zwolle.'

'You may get another good chance before the train gets up speed. Better take up positions again.'

We froze into our statuesque grouping. It was a nerve-racking business waiting for the moment. I should have been shaking had I been in Redman's shoes. It was difficult to believe it really was happening. But there was nothing unreal about my raised pulse-rate and dry mouth. It was a mere forty minutes since Apeldoorn and it had felt like hours.

Once more we reached open country. The train was still going quite slowly. Visibility was very limited. All to our advantage, and there was now a clear two feet of sand between the line and a narrow grass verge. Beyond this, on each side, was a shallow ditch with small bushes lining the top of its far bank.

Redman broke into our silence. 'This looks like it.' Then, to himself, urgently, 'Red light on. I'll be going. Green light. Now for it. GO.' With which he dropped neatly onto the verge and rolled out of sight into the ditch. As he went I gave the man next to me a sharp slap on his shoulder.

He hissed 'GO' to the corporal, who in turn disappeared from his side of the train. Looking back we could see no sign of life and I presumed each was lying doggo in his ditch. Again we watched and waited to see what reaction there might be from the Germans, and again there was none.

We had been six on the platform; now we were three. The next important step was to try to conceal the escapes as long as possible, not only to prevent information about them from being telephoned back down the line, but also to save ourselves from the reprisals we feared might be taken against us when and if we were found out. Back in the carriage we found the two surgeons continuing their performance, trying to convince the remaining, protesting padre that a blanket worn toga style was more becoming than a poncho. Curiosity had at length got the better of Franz, who had put down his book and left his bunk and was gazing in astonishment at the extravagant gestures of the actors. His face was a picture. I could imagine him saying to himself, 'these Englishmen are quite mad.' Smith raised his eyebrows at Alford who nodded. 'Carry on a bit longer,' he said, 'We don't want the penny to drop just yet.'

We had had our evening meal before Apeldoorn and so there was not too much risk of Franz's attention being focussed on the empty bunks and our absent friends. He was wont to count us, ponderously, before each meal, with up and down movements of his forefinger, ein, zwei, drei; presumably a convenient time for the roll call and to remind him of the needful number of rations. An aspect of the escape we had not taken into account, and now hit us forcefully, was the loss of Redman's ability as interpreter. All we had between us was a little schoolboy German, and I did not even have that. We played cards, while the train rattled on, and chatted and smoked, without a move from Franz until it was time to go to bed. Then he pointed to the empty bunks and said, rather plaintively,

'Wo sind der hauptmann und der pastor?'
Alford pointed emphatically in the direction of up the train and replied firmly,

'Mit kranks,' To fortify his meaning he came over to my bunkside, took my pulse, pulled out his stethoscope and listened to my chest, and gave me a thumbs up sign. Pointing up the train again he repeated, 'hauptmann and pastor mit kranks.'

Franz seemed satisfied, ambled off to his end of the compartment, and did nothing more that night.

The next morning was a different kettle of fish. As soon as he noticed the bunks were still empty Franz became very agitated, repeatedly putting the same question, and reeling off a lot of other remarks that left us none the wiser. We had already decided our best course lay in following Warrack's advice at Apeldoorn and to play 'daft laddie.' So we shrugged our shoulders, looked helpless and answered him with blank faced 'don't knows'. In fact it was the sober truth. We did not know where Theo and the padre were now. But what would Franz do next? He pushed past us and hurried out of the door.

'He's gone to look for them,' said Alford, 'and when he can't find them he's bound to tell the commandant.'

What else? We all agreed. The real music was sure to start soon. But when Franz eventually returned he was alone. He must have assumed they were not on the train because he bore with him rations but only enough for the six of us, and proceeded to prepare and distribute them, and then to get on with his own breakfast as if nothing questionable had happened. We had expected the commandant and trouble and all we had got was breakfast. I could not believe it.

'Must be a snag somewhere.'

'You can bet on that.'

'It's only a matter of time.'

'If I happened to be the commandant I'd be making my own search of the train.'

'He'll fetch up here sooner or later.'

Having travelled steadily during the night, without being aware of more than an occasional, brief halt we had the additional anxiety of not knowing exactly where we were. Were we still in Holland or in Germany? The train was moving fast over flat and uninteresting country.

'I think it must be Germany', said Alford. 'The farms are bigger and the architecture's different. It feels different. Going mainly east too.'

We had our heads down, engrossed in one of the pocket handkerchief escape kit maps, well concealed from Franz, in concentrated discussion when all at once heavy footsteps sounded on the metal platform. The map was safely whipped away seconds before the door was violently opened and the commandant appeared, red in the face, eyes glinting, with two of his staff at his heels. Franz leapt to his feet and stood stiffly to attention.

'Aufstehen,' he shouted, motioning us to our feet with his head. We complied, backing away from the menacing figure at the door. The commandant fixed his beady eyes on Franz, beckoning him forwards, then proceeded to hector him in a crescendo of angry tones. Franz visibly wilted and, to judge from my own feelings, none of us could have been feeling too good. Then the commandant transferred his baleful stare to us, and said something that resulted in one of his minions coming from behind to stand at his elbow to act, it was quickly apparent, as interpreter. The commandant bellowed,

'Where are the other officers?'
Alford advanced to the wicket to receive the bowling.
'I do not know.'
'They are not on the train.' No reply.
'They have escaped. You as senior British officer are responsible.'
'I do not know where they are.'
'When did you last see them?'
'Last night.'
'Why did you not report their absence?'
'I was asleep. I did not know until this morning they had not returned from visiting patients.'
The commandant's veins stood out on each side of his forehead.
'You are lying.'
'I do not know where they are'.
The commandant then launched into a furious tirade, while the interpreter injected fragments of his harangue into the loaded atmosphere at what only could have been his own discretion, as he was given no time to convey the whole.
'Liars.' 'gangsters.' 'Disobeyed explicit orders.' 'Not to be trusted.' 'Not gentlemen.' 'Should be shot.' So it went on. I was quaking but, as every doctor comes to learn; even the most verbose complainant, if listened to patiently and quietly, dries up in the end, and the end came eventually, with the commandant taking out a handkerchief and mopping his face.
His silence was, if anything, more unnerving than his noise. It was obvious he was making up his mind what to do with us. When the sentence came, delivered more in sorrow than anger, it was anticlimactic in its leniency.
I will permit you to visit your patients, but only once a day and only if accompanied by a guard. The rest of the time you will remain locked in this compartment.'
Alford, no doubt feeling this was well wide of his stumps, chanced an offensive stroke.
'It is understood Herr Commandant. Thank you. I assure you there will be no more officers going missing. I would wish to spare both of us the embarrassment. But might we not be permitted to visit our patents twice a day? There are so few of us and so much to do.'
The commandant looked hard at each one of us and then at Alford.
'I have your word there will be no further escape attempts?'
'You have.'
'Very well. It will be permitted. The matter is now closed. Heil Hitler.'
With which he turned on his heel and left the compartment.

Franz sadly and gloomily advanced on the door and locked it. We subsided onto our bunks.

'Never thought we would get off as lightly as that, sir,' I said brightly. Alford was pensive.

'My bet is,' he spoke slowly and judiciously, 'no-one outside of this train will ever get to hear of it. The commandant won't want to report the failure of his security. He'll fudge his figures. Theo and the padre will not appear on his nominal role.'

We digested this thought in silence. Then Smith said

'That will improve their chances no end.'

'Right. If they are not reported missing nobody will be looking for them.' On which cheerful note we resumed our discussion concerning our position on the map until, shortly, the guards came to the door to escort us individually up the train to visit our allotted patients.

The work was not now very onerous. Some of the seriously wounded were in very bad shape, especially those with head injuries, but all had received their definitive treatment at Apeldoorn. Fractures had been set and put in plaster, bullets and shell splinters had been removed from wounds, and tissues repaired. Blood losses had been made good, except in a few cases where drips were still going. It was mainly a question of assisting the healing processes with changes of dressings, administration of appropriate drugs, and morale-boosting words of comfort. But it was time-consuming. Every man in the train had to be seen and there were a lot of them. When I got back to the carriage Franz had the rations ready and I fell to with a will.

Not long after, when we were having a siesta on our bunks, the question of our whereabouts was answered by our arrival at the station of a large town with the name place, OLDENBURG, prominently on display. Thereafter we were able to plot our course, travelling first south, to Osnabruch, then south-east to Hanover, and then north, finally arriving at the station of Falingbostel on the morning of 9 October. The journey was over.

The thirty-six hours spent in the train had for me, in its later stages, bought well-needed time to make the mental adjustments consequent upon the acceptance of the end of all hope of liberation by the advancing second army and the certain prospect of internment. I had never taken into consideration the reality of being a prisoner of war, having in my mind but hazy pictures of barbed-wire compounds and grim looking fortresses. I was caught mentally unprepared and apprehensive and the train had helped. There was a novelty about it and I had been kept busy. It had not asked too much and stimulated the process of adaptation. I felt ready for the next phase, ready to agree with one of my companions who remarked,

'I've been most things as an MO in this war. This experience will top it off nicely.'

III

Falingbostel
(9 October – 16 November 1944)

The train had been standing in the station about an hour when the commandant appeared, and informed us we were to collect our belongings and assemble outside on the platform. His tone was affable and demeanour relaxed, obviously glad and relieved to have delivered us safely at our destination without further incident.

'I wish you the best of luck gentlemen,' he gave a little bow, 'you will have prolonged opportunities for practicing your profession here in Germany.' The interpreter emphasised the word prolonged. My God, I thought, he doesn't know he's lost the war and sees our internment as permanent. 'That is as long as you co-operate and comply strictly with our regulations. If not ...' He left the sentence in mid-air and treated us to a gold-filled toothy smirk. 'Heil Hitler.'

On the platform a German NCO was shouting, waving his arms, and strutting about trying to marshal the walking wounded and RAMC personnel into three ranks. It was a motley looking parade of gaunt-faced men in dirty, tattered battledresses, each festooned with sundry articles of personal gear, attached in many cases by untidy bits of string. I must have grown used to our unsavoury appearances while on the train because the sight of us all *en masse* came as quite a shock and it certainly was a very unprepossessing column that eventually set out painfully up

27

a cobbled road on what we were informed was to be a mere ten minute march. But we did our best to keep in step and carry ourselves straight.

The inhabitants of Falingbostel, going about their daily business, paid us little or no attention as we marched between the houses. I found this surprising considering the excitement a similar column of German prisoners would have occasioned in England. Later I came to understand the Germans were so used to having foreigners in their midst they took them for granted, especially here in the area of Falingbostel where I learned there were thousands, of all nationalities, either in camps or at work in factories and fields. To the Germans we were part of their normal backgound.

It was a warm, sunny morning, and we toiled wearily up a seemingly endless road which climbed steadily out of the town, really nothing more than a large agricultural village, into a countryside of fields and woods until we found ourselves within a belt of pinetrees. Here the column was allowed to fall out and rest for five minutes by the side of the road. The resinous smell of the pines took me straight back to the dropping zone at Arnhem, when we had paused in a similar locality after sorting ourselves out prior to beginning the abortive march to the bridge. Then we had been smiling and jaunty, groomed and smart, armed and fit, sure of our invincibility, too sure perhaps. There was no gainsaying we had come sadly to grief, and suffered a dismal reversal of fortune. I shrugged the thought away. No good dwelling on the glories of the past. Our present circumstances were undoubtedly depressing, more than that, menacing, for who could say what lay ahead. But one had to make the best of it all, taking everything as it came. Sufficient unto the day.

'Aufstehen. Aufstehen.' The German command that was to become as familiar and irritating as an alarm clock rang out harshly, and we clambered to our feet, shuffling ourselves morosely into our three ranks. Then once again we set off, the promised ten-minute walk already an hour old. We passed beneath a modern single-span concrete bridge, carrying another road over us, with a machine-gun emplacement at one end of it. Away on our right was a huge grim-looking building, resembling a block of women's flats in the worst dreariest taste. Our prison to be? No. On we went for another quarter of an hour until an obvious prisoner of war camp took shape on our left, announced by wooden watch-towers set at intervals along a high, double fence of barbed wire. Within the wire were numerous wooden huts, and knots of men here and there discernible in strange garments. The whole encampment looked enormous and I, placed at the head of the column with the other officers, experienced a feeling of dread as the gates hove into view. They, like the fence, were double, so that it was necessary to pass through two pairs of gates, each with two sentry boxes, and between two watch towers, one on each side equipped with searchlights and machine-guns, in order to enter or leave the camp. On the outer gate was attached a wooden board bearing the inscription:

M.STAMLAGER Xl B
FALINGBOSTEL

After negotiations and exchanges of paper between our guards and those on the gates we were marched inside. I looked round at the tail of the column and saw the last man in and the gates closed behind him. It was a bad moment. We were no more prisoners in the technical sense than we had been at Apeldoorn or on the train, but this passing within the barbed wire barrier had the psychological effect of symbolising a total surrender of liberty, of dividing the world into two groups, those outside and those inside, and I already had the strongest possible desire to get out. But it was a time for hiding one's personal feelings, for solidarity with one's companions. Colonel Alford strode doggedly in the centre of the front rank, with Major Smith on his right and myself on his left, following a German sergeant who urged us on with peremptory beckoning gestures. We were marching up a broad path between wooden huts towards a large building set in an open space, followed by the apathetic gaze of numerous prisoners in the uniforms of different nationalities, French and Belgian predominating. The British were wholly conspicuous by their absence. Smith said to Alford,

'Doesn't the Geneva Covention say each nationality should be segregated in separate camps? Aren't all British prisoners supposed to go to exclusively British camps?'

'Yes. I thought so.'

'Then what in the name of fortune are we doing here?'

We soon found out. We were halted, standing at ease outside the large building, awaiting events, when a small party of airborne British came by swinging empty billycans. There was an immediate breaking of ranks and a searching of faces for recognition, amid a babel of exclamations and questions. Alford singled out an NCO.

'Good to see you corporal. What sort of place is this?'

'Lousy, if you will excuse the expression, sir.'

'Been here long?'

'A week.'

'Many British here?'

'About a couple of hundred.'

'But it looks a big camp.'

'It is. But mostly full of Frogs and Russkis. They call it a corrective stalag for all nationalities.'

'You mean it's a punishment camp,' Alford commented.

'Well, sir, it's no Butlins. All rotten spuds and cabbage soup.'

'And this building here?'

'Concert hall I think, sir. We were taken in it for search and interrogation.'

By now both groups were hopelessly mixed up and the Germans were becoming exasperated, prodding threateningly with their rifles in an effort to restore some semblance of order. Eventually they succeeded in reforming the cookhouse party, which proceeded on its way, as pleased to have encountered us as we them. So this was a correction camp. A good beginning.

The concert hall had a big double-door entrance. The officers were held back in a small group on the right and taken in singly. The other ranks shuffled in on the left in a continuous queue. When it came to my turn I was met by a tall cheerful, fresh-faced British padre who announced,

'I'm padre to this camp. I'll stand by when they search you and see they don't pull any fast ones.'

'Why have they brought us here Padre?' I queried. 'We've been told it's a correction camp.'

'It's to do with an order that went out from Hitler after your battle. You're all regarded as potentially dangerous trouble makers. I afraid they'll keep you on a very tight rein.'

We advanced to a table at which was seated an elderly, somewhat cross-eyed German corporal who, surprisingly after what the padre had just said, submitted me to the most perfunctory inspection, merely standing up, leaning across the table and patting my uniform pockets. I had, on the padre's advice, already handed him my torch and clasp knife as items forbidden in the camp, and all he demanded now was my money, Dutch and German notes issued to me in England before take-off, for which he gave me a receipt. The padre said something to him in German and I was waved away.

'What was that?'

'I was just telling him on your behalf that you possessed nothing else you were not entitled to under the Geneva Convention.'

The padre then pointed me in the direction of the officers who had preceded me, gathered at the other end of the hall. I was amazed. It had been easier than peacetime British customs. He had not even turned out my haversack. None of us had had a proper body search. Just as well. There were still items of our escape kits on our persons, tiny compasses, small metal files and the printed pocket handkerchief maps.

'Not too bad so far,' said Smith.

I mentioned what the padre had said about Hitler and the tight rein. Smith responded with a puckish smile.

'Whoa? Is it then? Or is it Waho?' The point went home at once and we shouted gleefully as one,

'Waho Mohammed. Waho Mohammed,' which is the battle-cry of the 1st Airborne Division adopted when in its infancy in Tunisia. Our shout brought answering responses from all the British in the hall, including those beginning to be brought in on stretchers.

'Waho Mohammed. Waho Mohammed.'

The padre came swiftly over to our group and addressed himself urgently to Alford.

'I don't know what all this is about, sir,' he said anxiously, 'but you had better cool it. The Germans'll think it's a signal for some kind of riot, and there could be real unpleasantness.

A German sergeant major was already striding purposefully in our direction, shouting, 'Silence! Silence! Stille! Silence!' while the guards were fingering their rifles.

'It's nothing to worry about padre. We're only letting off steam.' Alford thoughtfully tugged at his moustache, 'tell him we were just applauding the arrival of the stretcher cases. Tell him we were cheering the Germans for bringing us all together again. Tell him anything.'

The sergeant major was by now stamping his feet and angrily bellowing for quiet. The padre spoke to him earnestly in German with an obvious mollifying effect. The sergeant addressed himself to Alford in passably good English,

'Please to order this to cease.'

I sensed something significant bearing on balance of authority in prisoner of war life was occurring. So I think did Alford. He allowed the hubbub to continue a moment or two longer then said to the sergeant, 'certainly.' After another pause he raised his voice, which rang loud and clear through the hall

'All right men. That's enough.'

There was an immediate hush. Alford smiled affably at the sergeant major. The sergeant major, a thin-lipped, blond, rugged-faced man of some thirty years gave him a hard stare back, then abruptly pulled a note-book out of his tunic pocket. Pointing in the direction of the stretcher cases, who all this time had been piling up in the hall, dumped unceremoniously on the floor by bearers detailed from among the French population of prisoners, he said,

'The Oberstabsarzt wishes all patients to be moved at once to the camp lazaret. You must sort, sortieren. Badly wounded to the beds first.'

An oberstabsarzt was a medical officer with the rank of major, and a lazaret an infirmary or hospital. These orders struck an optimistic note for us. It looked as if the medical services at least were going to afford us proper facilities, and we moved eagerly among the stretchers, listing priorities and cheering the wounded, telling them they would soon be in comfortable beds getting good treatment and food.

We were about half way through this task when a loud shout of 'achtung' and a stamping of feet coming to attention drew our eyes to the door. Conversation with the wounded trailed off as a small group of German officers approached, directed by the sergeant major towards Alford to whom we also instinctively gravitated. The foremost of the German officers was a fat man with a pink complexion and beady little eyes. He was big, over six foot, wore ill-fitting breeches tucked into black jack-boots to which were attached large-rowelled spurs, and on his shoulders bore the silver epaulettes of a major. He came to a standstill before us, quite a formidable figure, casually removing some gloves, while the sergeant announced,

'Attention please. You are in the presence of Chefarzt of the camp. Herr Oberstabsarzt Möglich. He wishes to meet you in turn. Please to stand before him one by one in order of seniority, and announce your name and rank.' Following this little ceremony Möglich made a short speech, translated by the sergeant between dramatic pauses, to the effect that he hoped we would cooperate with him, since the work of doctors should be unaffected by the disputes of nations. Then, without further ado, he strode away towards the group of French prisoners who, having carried in the stretchers, were hanging about by the door. When all the other Germans, who followed him, were out of earshot the padre said very quietly,

'Möglich is the German word for possible. But I should warn you, I very much fear you will find him impossible. Look! What's he up now?'

Möglich, followed by the French, was moving down the lines of stretchers and, quite arbitrarily, without attempting to assess severity of wounds, picking out patients and ordering the French to carry them out. It was farcical. Our careful classification was going by the board. Somebody in a plaster of paris splint, perhaps with a minor fracture, would catch his eye and off he would be taken, while a grey-faced man with an abdominal wound apparently asleep was totally ignored.

Alford grabbed the padre by the arm and advanced on Möglich with the rest of us at his heels.

'Tell him I strongly protest. Tell him we have the lists prepared as he ordered and I can say exactly who should be the first to receive whatever medical benefits there are on offer.'

The padre cleared his throat and hesitatingly translated. Möglich kept his back to us and continued on his ponderous way without a word.

'Tell him again' said Alford indignantly, 'shout at him if necessary. The padre shot Alford a warning look, opened his mouth as if to say something, appeared to change his mind and, once again in a firmer voice reaimed Alfords message at Möglich's back. This time Möglich rounded on us, his beady eyes glinting in anger. There was an explosion of German accompanied by a beating of his right fist, clenched round his gloves, into his left palm. Then he stormed out of the hall to an accompaniment of heel clicking and Heil Hitlers.

'Well?' Alford looked at the padre, who had a rueful told-you-so expression on his face.

'It's not a good start. Möglich's message is that you will soon discover it is not customary for prisoners of war to criticise the actions of German officers.

Out of the corner of my eye I saw a familiar figure approaching.

'Watch out. Here comes the sergeant major.'

We braced ourselves for more trouble, but the sergeant was all peace and pleasantry.

'It is better you always come to me with questions,' he said with an ingratiating smile and pointing his forefinger at his chest,

'My name is Niebling. I will do for you whatever I can. Do not trouble the Chefarzt with requests. I can arrange things. We will move the rest of the wounded to the lazaret now as you wish. If you have patients who need to go to hospital I will have ambulances take them to Hanover.'

Before the full import of his last words had sunk in he quickly went on to suggest that some of us should immediately go down to the lazaret to organise the reception of the wounded. Alford voiced the disquiet now mounting within.

'Is not the lazaret a hospital?' He looked at Niebling, then at the padre.

'The best one here.' said Niebling. The padre looked embarrassed.

'I don't like the sound of things at all,' Alford commented, 'the sooner we get down there the better,' then, turning to me, 'will you stay here until the last man's out. You can speak the Frog's lingo, and supervise the stretcher bearing.'

'I'll stay with him,' volunteered the padre, 'when we're through I'll nobble a guard and bring him down to you. OK?'

'Fine.'

Between us the padre and I were able to direct the evacuation of the hall without undue difficulty, and without interference from the Germans. There were relays of French constantly replenishing the bearer parties, who bore their burdens with a drooping air of resignation, yet with care enough to avoid jolting the patients. At length the last man was lifted. The padre beckoned a guard, I gathered up my gear and we went out into the sunshine.

'Tell me what Niebling meant about the hospital at Hanover.' I searched the padre's face as we walked along.

'I can tell you now the lazaret's a dump. Just a dump to accommodate sick and wounded and no way are the Germans going to put you anywhere else today. I feared if I told your colonel the truth there would be a fruitless row. You've a tough time ahead.'

We were approaching a large compound surrounded by its own barbed wire fence.

'This is it.'

I began to see what he meant. Within the wire were a series of low rectangular wooden huts each, again, separately enclosed by its own barbed wire fence. We entered the compound through a sentry-guarded gate, adjacent to which was a larger hut with a veranda and a guard at the door-step.

'Chefarzt Möglich's HQ.' The padre nodded at it. 'You'll be seeing more of that I shouldn't wonder.'

Another few hundred yards and we followed the stretcher into one of the huts.

'This is where I get off.' said the padre.

'Thanks for all your help.'

Pip Smith was in the passage. He pointed me to the first door on the left.

'Put your stuff in there. Any vacant bunk. Then join me.'

It was a tiny room, about ten feet square, furnished with four double tier bunks, a table, a few stools and a bank of eight small wooden cupboards. In one corner stood a stove, and the only window looked out onto the barbed wire surround, a dirt path, more barbed wire and another similar hut. The bunks had straw mattresses on wooden boards, a straw-filled pillow, one blanket and a blue-and-white chequered sheet.

The corridor was now deserted. Several doors opened off it. I looked into the first and rocked back onto my heels. It was crammed full of our men in double-tier bunks. Five bunks down each side, one at the far end, twenty two men in a room not much more than eight paces long and five paces wide, with a low ceiling and shut fast windows. All the so-called wards were the same. This was no hospital. We'd been sold down the river. Smith was seeing to a patient. I helped him with the bandage.

'I just can't believe it,' I gasped at him, 'did they really take all that trouble with the hospital train just to bring us to this? It's incomprehensible.'

'They did and they have.' Smith must already have come to terms with his own indignation. He turned to practical matters. 'First thing we've to do here is to get the men all comfortably bedded down. Then, Niebling says, there'll be a meal. Alford wants us all back in the mess for a conference as soon as possible.

'Mess is the right word for it.' I commented bitterly. It was about four o'clock in the afternoon when we assembled under Alford. At Niebling's direction cookhouse parties had been formed from the RAMC orderlies to collect rations, and he had told Alford if we submitted a list of our medical requirements he would arrange for them to be issued from the pharmacy before the day was out. We sat round the table and started to compile a list. We had no medical supplies at all, apart from the negligible small items we had managed to conserve and carry with us, and so it was a long one. Then we had a council of war. Alford had seen the padre again and learned a lot more. There were in fact about fifty other non-airborne British in the camp and, by a stroke of good luck, two airborne MOs who had been captured at Arnhem and brought here several days ahead of us. They had been working against appalling difficulties but had begun to make headway and find out the 'ropes'. The camp had been in existence for some years and was populated mainly with French, Yugoslav and Russian prisoners. The French had been here the longest and, consequently, had more or less cornered the running of the camp from the prisoners' angle. There were French cooks in the cookhouse, seven French doctors in the lazaret compound, and they were well supplied with Red Cross parcels. The camp currency was cigarettes, packets of which came in the parcels. Everything had a purchase value. A loaf of bread could be had for a packet of twenty, a pot of jam for as many, and other items of food had their standard price. Even coal for heating the huts was purchasable; and the French ran the bath house. More than that the Gemans were susceptible to cigarette, coffee or chocolate bribes. The rub was we British, the latest arrivals, were at a distinct disadvantage. We had no parcels, no coffee, chocolate or cigarettes with which to barter, while, by now, other nationalities, with the exception of the Russians, whose government did not recognise the Red Cross nor subscribe to the Geneva Convention, were well supplied and able to supplement the meagre daily rations with extra commodities. Since this ration was totally inadequate to do more than just support life, these extras made the difference between a tolerable or desperately miserable existance. Alford concluded.

'So that's it. We'll leave it now and see where we are tomorrow. Somehow we've got to get on top of things. We'll hold a council of war every evening and collate all the information we've managed to gather during the day. The thing is to get ourselves properly organised and demand our rights.'

The rations arrived in buckets, cabbage soup in one lot, unpeeled black-eyed boiled potatoes in the other, as earlier predicted. We busied ourselves with the distribution of this exotic fare which was wolfed down by the hungry wounded without even a pause for ribald comment. Those with abdominal injuries who should have been on special diets, and had been the hospital train, were in a parlous state. The best we could do for them was to clean up and mash some of the potatoes. But they could not take much and it was not going to sustain them.

Niebling came and took our list, pursing his lips as he took in its length. It was getting dark and he looked significantly at the window.

'I regret gentlemen the pharmacy is closed. I also regret I must now have you locked up for the night. The lights will go out at twenty-one hundred hours. Nobody must attempt to leave the building. Any prisoner found outside will unfortunately incur the penalty of being shot. I wish you a good night. Sleep well.'

Sleep well? Why not? It had been a long day and was a dreadful place but we were in one piece, individually and collectively, and were very tired. We slept.

At five-thirty next morning the lights came on, there was the sound of the hut being unlocked. Our door was thrown open and in stamped a German guard, eyeing us distastefully.

'Aufstehen.' 'Raus.' 'Raus.' 'Alles heraus.'

The harsh voice left me in no doubt of its meaning.

'Aufstehen.' 'Schnell.'

I was lying in the bunk above Captain Ian Huddlestone, co-surgeon of Pip Smith, who showed no disposition whatever to move. I leant over and touched him on the shoulder.

'They want us to get up, I think,' I said.

He opened one eye and fixed me with a baleful stare.

'They can go to hell.'

I subsided back onto my bunk being entirely inclined to agree with him. But the guard came into the room and shook us roughly with more shouts of 'raus'. Nothing for it but to comply.

There was a washroom at the far end of the hut to which we made our way to relieve ourselves and scrape painfully at our faces. I was thankful I still had my Rolls razor as it could be sharpened afresh for each shave, for the bars of ersatz soap and cold water provided did little to soften the stubble.

The day was before us. A day of unremitting work. With the two already resident MOs we now had a medical staff of seven to look after the wounded accommodated into the three adjacent barrack huts allotted to us. These were the serious cases that had to be nursed in bed, twenty-two to a 'ward' in double bunks as described, six wards to a hut. Each hut had had one small room set aside for dressings and minor operations. The only water to be had was in the washroom, and the rooms were filthy. After the distribution of 'breakfast', ersatz coffee and two slices of black bread. We set about our various tasks. Smith and I were to work in this hut, Huddlestone and another MO in the next, two others in the third. The remaining MO, one of the earlier arrivals who had a smattering of German, stayed alongside Alford, who intended, after a detailed inspection and assessment of our situation, to visit the Chefarzt with a catalogue of demands, and try to contact the other medical nationals in the lazaret compound.

Medical work at this time with the wounded was, from our point of view, routine, repetitive and, thankfully, undramatic. We had had all the drama we wanted in the battle. It was now, and would continue to be, a matter of keeping wounds clean by changing of dressings, replacing pus-softened plaster-of-Paris splints, building up resistance to infection and sustaining the healing processes. Sometimes sequestra, pieces of dead bone, had to be removed and abscesses drained under an anaesthetic. The main problems were the overcrowding and inadequate diet compounded by lack of antibiotics and pain-killing drugs.

I had only to go into a 'ward' and see the shocking conditions uncomplainingly endured by the wounded men to know myself to be very fortunate by comparison. It is ever thus with doctoring. At the beginning there is often fear. A medical student's first contact with a vile or hideous disease, and exposure to new knowledge of the mode of onset, early symptoms and signs of recognition can trigger off anxious imaginings. I recall being shown an unfortunate patient with advanced pulmonary tuberculosis, very rare these days. The consultant had him sitting up in bed stripped to the waist. We students took it in turn to listen to his emaciated chest.

'Note,' said the consultant, 'how much lower his right shoulder is than his left. That is because the lung on that side is hardly working at all.'

I spent the afternoon playing rugby football without giving another thought to Tb. But next morning, washing and shaving, I suddenly noticed in the mirror an asymmetry of my own shoulder lines – right lower than left. The panic welled up unbidden. Oh my God I've got it! I spent a miserable two days repeatedly examining myself in the mirror. At last I could stand it no longer and went to my Medical Tutor, fearful lest he should confirm my own diagnosis. He had the wisdom to treat my neurotic anxiety with the utmost gravity, submitting me to a time-consuming searching examination, first of my recollection of past illnesses and symptoms and then of my person.

'You were quite right to come to me.' My heart missed a beat. 'You never know. But I can assure you you are absolutely A1.' Then with a smile, 'many people have an asymmetry of some kind. Have you, by chance, ever noticed how very rarely a person's two ears are exactly matched on each side?'

Relief flooded over me. I smiled back sheepishly. 'Thank you sir,' I said, 'I hope I won't trouble you again.'

'You won't.'

And I didn't. Since that day I have always found it possible to concern myself deeply with any patient, however objectively distressed the complaint, untrammelled by self-concern arising from a psychological transference of situation. This is the detachment, sometimes mistaken for callousness, necessary for calm and effective ministration. It was, I believe, an important milestone that absolutely confirmed me in my choice of career, one that has meant the acceptance of my own complete unexemption from all the 'ills frail flesh is heir to,' and sometimes I wish I didn't know there were so many and so much about them, but, over and above, the enjoyment of a steady satisfaction in the attempt to restore and reclaim health for others, enhanced by the salutary perspective contemplation of their lot gives to one's own.

The council of war that evening was attended by the padre who had welcomed us on our arrival and the British Man-of-confidence, camp leader of the other, non-airborne, British prisoners. Alford began by recounting his own activities. Möglich had been unavailable and Niebling unforthcoming, but useful contacts had been made with other nationals together with a general reconnoitre of the camp. The Yugoslavs had been the most positive in offers of help. One of their surgeons had promised gifts of parcels, cigarettes, clothing and blankets, and had placed his operating theatre at our disposal. The Belgians had passed on cigarettes to give to our men and been as helpful as their own situation permitted, but they were not very numerous and could not do much. The Russians were totally isolated in their own separate compound and were very badly off. According to the creed of Nazi officialdom they were 'untermenschen', subhuman, and were kept deliberately in an ill-clad, starving, insanitary and disease-ridden condition commensurate with this crude, crooked-cross Swastika concept. Other nationalities, particularly the French, took up a friendly, but firmly business-like attitude. They would trade if we had the wherewithal to trade back. In their view that was what the camp life was all about.

'So,' Alford concluded, 'that is the general situation. Not too promising. I think I was right in insisting on putting our requirements directly to Möglich. Niebling wanted to short-cut me and said he would obtain the things. But I pointed out he hadn't yet produced the stuff he had promised from the pharmacy. He didn't like it much. Went off in a huff.'

The Man-of-Confidence raised a hand. 'Permission to speak, sir?'

'Of course.'

'Niebling is not on any account to be trusted. We have found him viciously tempered and totally unreliable. His promises are worthless.'

The padre nodded in agreement, 'I would say that's right. One of the worst. But don't trust any of them. Don't try to wheedle or barter. The only way to deal with the Germans is to insist loudly on your rights under the Geneva Convention, to demand they accord you the treatment that is yours by right under the agreed usages of war, and ...'

'never forgetting,' Alford continued the sentence for him, 'we are part of a victorious army, not prisoners from a beaten country demoralised by years of captivity. We must carry on the fight. We must be smartly turned out and disciplined; spit and polish and a soldierly bearing at all times to maintain our self-respect. I've been told it's the German policy in this camp to try to break a prisoner's spirit from the start by keeping him on short rations and harrying him from pillar to post. But I have the advantage of rank over Möglich and intend to use it.'

Alford was warming up, banging the table with his fist to emphasise his points. The padre let fall a cool word of caution.

'Don't overplay the rank, sir. It's a good card and can be very useful at the right time. But Möglich will have you posted elsewhere at the drop of a hat if he is made to feel at all inferior.'

'I take the point,' said Alford, looking at Smith upon whose shoulders the senior rôle would fall in this event. Smith looked pensive, his somewhat domed forehead creased, his brows drawn together, his eyes down apparently studying something on the table. Then he looked up at Alford and spoke in his usual deliberate, mild and almost gentle way,

'I say fight the bastards. Use whatever influence your rank serves while you can. Press for what we need now. It's a hand to mouth existence anyway. We can only live from day to day. I have to worry about what happens if they move you when and if it happens.'

We studied a copy of the Geneva Convention the padre had brought with him and noted exactly what our prisoner-of-war rights were, especially with regard to the sick and wounded, and learned how to apply for redress by writing to the Red Cross headquarters or to the protecting power. It was agreed Alford would insist on seeing Möglich first thing in the morning and demand more medical orderlies to work in the lazaret, more space for the patients, more blankets, more food, more coal, facilities for X-rays and so on. We agreed an effort would have to be made to oust the French from their total monopoly of the cookhouse and get one or more of our own men in to look after our interests. We worked ourselves up to a fine pitch of indignation and everyone felt much the better for it. The next morning we were brought down to earth.

At 8 o'clock Niebling appeared, several henchmen at his heels, and announced that he intended to inspect the wards. Good, thought I for one, perhaps we shall begin to get somewhere. But I was quickly disabused of such wishful thinking. Niebling stormed into each of the wards preceded by a corporal shouting 'achtung' and 'stille', 'attention', 'silence'. Niebling found fault everywhere. The wards were dirty, men unshaven, smell unspeakable. He was enraged because the patients were wearing clothes, full battledress in many cases, in bed, despite the weather having turned very cold and there being insufficient blankets to go round two to each man. Alford of course protested, said the conditions were not of our making, and pinned Niebling down about the non-arrival of the supplies from the pharmacy, and asked him why we had heard no more about the ambulances to take the seriously wounded to the fine hospital in Hanover. Niebling's voice shook with anger.

'Your RAF bandits have bombed it!' he shouted.

Alford ignored this reply and simply said in a quiet but hard voice 'I am a lieutenant colonel in the British army. You are a sergeant major in the German army. The German army is losing the war. I demand to see Major Möglich and,' he went on while we held our breath, 'you will kindly afford me the courtesy of standing to attention when I address you.'

Niebling shot him a look of pure, killing hatred. But it worked. 'Very well. Come.'

Niebling's English was reasonably good and these exchanges were without the intermediary of an interpreter. Interpreters were all very well if they were from our side, but generally the Germans used theirs, and if there were no German-speaking British present things could go awry through unmonitored misrepresentation.

Apprehensively Smith and I awaited Alford's return to the hut, wondering all the while how he was getting on with Möglich. To offset this anxiety we had our work, more than enough to keep us occupied. Rebandaging was a problem as we were right out of linen and cotton wool and had to make do with strips of paper and dried moss, all the Germans had so far given us. Other nationals had told us the Germans were genuinely short of many medical essentials, or what we would regard as essentials, and it was beginning to dawn on us that as they were having to improvise so would we – perhaps indefinitely. Alford duly returned, in quite good heart as Möglich had at least listened to everything he had to say, and he thought he had managed to disentangle from the inevitable ensuing bluster an intimation of intention on Möglich's part to do what he could to make up some of the deficiencies. But Niebling was not finished with us yet.

Later on that day he arrived accompanied by the Camp Control Officer, a Nazi official responsible for the allocation of work, housing, feeding and general management of prisoners in the camp. He was a small, scrawny man in a black uniform, head shaven Prussian style, with very narrow set eyes and a beaky nose, on which were clipped gold-rimmed pince-nez glasses, a complete contrast to the burly Niebling who towered over him but obviously held him in great respect. Niebling made the introductions, and then stepped aside to make way for the official camp interpreter.

'Herr Lieutenant Colonel', the Control Officer began, placing himself casually in front of Alford with his hands on his hips, 'I have received an unfortunate complaint,' the smirk on Niebling's face left no doubt as to its source, 'concerning the state of your wards. I am told they are exceedingly dirty. Not at all what I would expect from your medical corps. I understand your army very much prides itself on its standards of hygiene?' He leaned back awaiting the effect of his words, no doubt anticipating an abject apology. But Alford had already had enough, and barked back at him.

'We have only been here a bare forty-eight hours. I was assured before we left Apeldoorn our wounded would be taken to proper hospitals and receive treatment as good as that given to German soldiers. Instead of which we have been crammed into these already filthy huts, with no facilities for proper care and only one broom for each hut. All our wounded have had an exhausting and painful time and been in need of our urgent attention. We have not had the opportunity to clean the place up, even if we had the means.' He paused while this was translated and, before the German could reply, continued in a parade-ground voice, 'you supply us with more orderlies, more medical supplies and more brooms, and you will no doubt find an improvement in the state of our wards if you care to visit us at a later date.'

The Control Officer's eyes narrowed and he clipped his pince-nez more firmly onto his nose. 'There are rules which prisoners-of-war must obey,' he snapped, 'it is for your own good that I insist, *insist*, on an immediate improvement in the state of your wards. I am not a doctor,' Alford grimly nodded his agreement, 'but I know well enough dirty rooms are unhealthy and do not give wounded men the best chance.'

The confrontation was now irrevocably joined and hotting up in earnest. Alford riposted.

'Then perhaps you also know overcrowded conditions and lack of proper medical facilities give wounded men no chance at all. I repeat, I demand to know why they were brought here in the first place, instead of to a proper hospital. The Geneva Convention insists our wounded should receive the same treatment as yours. Why has this not been observed?'

The Control Officer dropped his nonchalant pose, and removing his hands from his hips he dropped one onto the butt of his pistol and pointed the other at Alford. 'Because' he said icily, 'your bestial air force has bombed all the hospitals in Hanover and Brunswick and other German towns, and we have not enough hospitals even for our own men.'

'In that case,' replied Alford evenly, 'if there is inadequate hospital accommodation in Germany why were our wounded not repatriated or at least left in Holland where they were better off than they are here?'

The Control Officer, ignoring this point, took a menacing step foreward and fairly shouted, 'you talk of the Geneva Convention and yet your air force bombs hospitals and civilians. Why? Why? Answer me that.'

There was a brief silence before Alford spoke, and I had a feeling the encounter was beginning to get out of hand.

'I take it,' said Alford, while we instinctively grouped ourselves closer to him, 'you must have forgotten the German Air Force bombed cities like Warsaw, Rotterdam, London and Coventry quite regardless of the deaths of civilians and destruction of hospitals?'

'That is a lie!' shouted the Control Officer, 'another foul Allied lie. Those raids were all aimed at military targets. But your raids are savage, murderous, inhuman. You want to wipe out our cities and kill our women and children and ...' Alford interrupted the sweating interpreter, shouting back in turn,

'What about the women and children killed and the towns wiped out in Poland, France, Belgium, Holland and Russia ...' he was falling over his words in indignation, 'when your army attacked them without provocation. Your army began this war.'

'You began this war!' The Control Officer's voice reached the top of a crescendo, 'began this war at Versailles. You began it in nineteen eighteen.'

I was not the only one thinking Alford might be about to hit the ceiling. Smith laid a restraining hand on his arm and spoke very quietly into his ear. 'This is getting nowhere. He'll be on about Frederick the Great and Napoleon next. If he completely loses his temper we could really get it in the neck. It needs cooling.'

'OK', said Alford out of the corner of his mouth, 'I'll try to cool it.' He took a deep breath. 'Please,' he said in a placatory tone of voice, 'let us not concern ourselves with nineteen eighteen. Our concern is for the wounded here and now, in this lazaret. You surely cannot blame us if we try to obtain every possible advantage for them?'

The Control Officer's wrath appeared to abate. He opened and closed his mouth a few times without uttering, rocking back and forth on his heels, then said with finality, turning to leave and throwing the words over his shoulder,

'And you must not blame us if we cannot give them every possible advantage.'

'Whew' said Huddlestone, 'Well done Sir. Won that round I reckon.'

'Yes, well done Sir,' we all chimed in. But I had a feeling of anticlimax, of stalemate.

'It's the fanatical politics that gets me,' I hesitated, 'easy to be wise after the event. But if they really believe all that about Versailles this war's been inevitable for a long time; as long as they've had this griev-ance. My Father told me he thought Hitler wouldn't be such a fool as to start a second world war, and then there were the newspapers saying it couldn't last more than six months. I find it very depressing. They still don't understand they're beaten.'

'Well they are,' said Alford brusquely, 'they bloody well are, and you can cheer up. They may be short of things but I'm taking my demands up to the Chefarzt every damn morning 'til he does something.'

The first week at M. Stamlager X1 B was certainly no picnic. We were underfed, overworked, baulked at every turn by our captors, and disad-vantaged as newcomers to the camp by our relative poverty, and igno-rance of the black market protocol. The condition of many, if not most, of the patients deteriorated; they lost weight, wound infections worsened and the wards stank of putrefaction. There was insufficient fuel to heat the rooms properly and cold became another tormentor. But Alford persisted in his daily demands, a steady drip of pressure on the stony Möglich that by degrees brought us visible signs of some indentation. For during the second week there were improvements. We had needed plaster of Paris and we were given some, nothing like enough but at least something to go on with. We needed X-ray facilities and were allowed a small quota of takes. We needed extra food and were allocated a few Red Cross and invalid diet parcels. We received presents of cigarettes from neighbouring British prisoners through the intermediation of the padre, who was permitted to travel the Falingbostel circuit of camps to minister to his flock. This improved our bargaining position on the 'market', and enabled us to negotiate with the French and introduce a reliable man of our own to the cookhouse; an important move as he could supervise our ration issue. No longer were our ration orderlies obliged to accept buckets left over after others had taken their pick, nor entertain doubts about short-weighting. But the end of the second week also brought a sad blow. Alford returned from one of his interviews with Möglich looking grim.

'I'm being posted. Leaving tomorrow for another camp. God knows where.'

'Oh no!' The chorus was spontaneous. 'Why?'

'I expect I've leaned on him too heavily for his liking, as the padre warned might happen. It'll be up to you now Pip.'

Smith looked as though he had just put something extremely distasteful into his mouth. Alford went on,

'I might as well tell you what view I've come to take of Möglich, the sort of man we're having to deal with. First and foremost I've concluded he is a convinced and dedicated Nazi, or at any rate the party has the clamps on him. Second, I suspect he's an ignorant doctor by our standards but conceals it well. He's shrewd. He goes round the lazaret and listens to what one lot of doctors tell him about their treatments, then moves to another group and tries to impress them with his knowledge. He doesn't like his job, I'm sure of that, as in all our conversations I've never detected any real feelings of concern for the patients. Perhaps he's been put here because he's no use, not good enough for the front. Perhaps he feels he's been downgraded. He certainly seems to have a chip on his shoulder. He takes whatever it is out on everybody including his own staff, especially Niebling. He likes to rule by fear. In fact being feared, I would say, is the only thing he really enjoys. But he also likes to be thought 'correct'. I've hammered away at him on the correctness of the treatment he should be affording us, quoted the Convention *ad nauseum*, and I've also let drop a few hints that when the Allies arrive here he could be very glad of a good report from me on his conduct. I think that's where I went wrong. He doesn't really believe in an Allied victory.'

'Silly bugger.' muttered Smith.

'And', concluded Alford, 'as there is no knowing quite how long you will be in his power I would soft-pedal on that line, and try buttering him up a bit. Tell him what a good doctor you think he is. Tell him you understand about the shortages, but have confidence in his good will and ability to get us what we need. But he's moody. Most of the time you'll have to play it by ear.'

As Smith and the rest of us absorbed these words of wisdom from the only one among us who had regularly, daily, stood toe-to-toe with the

Chefarzt, I began to realise what a loss Alford's departure was going to be. Smith was of the same rank as Möglich and theoretically would be able to negotiate on equal terms. But Alford, having been commanding officer of a Parachute Field Ambulance had an air about him of habitual authority that generated an unsolicited response of respect, even from the enemy. Smith's testing time was upon him. I was glad it was not to be me.

We saw Alford off in the morning with heavy hearts and then Smith took over. It has been said that no sailor knows whether he has it in him to be a captain until he is given a ship. Smith had it in him. He rose to the occasion without hesitation.

'OK boys, I'm off to see Möglich. I'll ask the bloody man how the hell he thinks we can dress wounds properly with the present piddling issue of paper bandages, and see if I can get him to cough up some more plaster and bed-pans. Keep your fingers crossed for me.'

He stumped off, a picture of pugnacious resentment. I only hoped he would not hit his own stumps in the bat-swinging mood he was in. Now he was vexed not only by the problems arising out of his responsiblities as senior surgeon in clinical charge of treatment, but with the additional burdensome role of overall administrator and chief negotiator for our section of the lazaret. It was a tough assignment and we all felt for him. He had intended visiting our other huts after Möglich and it was not until we were all assembled in our mess for the midday meal that he returned, surprising us all by giving the thumbs up sign and wearing a cheerful, albeit somewhat puzzled, expression on his face.

He sat down at the table and we waited for him to tell us.

'I can't believe it. Möglich clapped me on the shoulder, and said "yes" to everything I asked him. Went on all about the "happy cooperation we doctors should enjoy in looking after the welfare of the wounded". I was quite prepared for any kind of showdown, but he was all affability and concession. Quite took the wind out of my sails.'

'He's up to something.' said Huddleston. 'Softening you up for some more bad news I shouldn't wonder.'

'Nor would I, in the least,' Smith went on, 'but it didn't feel like it. We'll never know exactly how much of an aggravation Bill Alford was to him. He may feel assuaged for the time being by having rid of him.'

'Proof of the pudding'll be in the eating.' I ventured, and then wished I hadn't.

'There'll be no bloody pudding, of that you can be sure,' spluttered Huddleston, 'but there are men here who could damn well do with some. Decent rice-pudding instead of the dirty potato peelings and ersatz coffee muck nobody can live on.'

There was, indeed, no pudding, but things did improve. Niebling appeared later that same day, all smug smiles, with supplies of plaster of Paris, paper bandages and diet parcels. By the end of the third week wounds were healing and men were getting up and about, some had even been discharged from the lazaret. We had made a start on occupational therapy, getting the men onto needlework, patching and repairing clothes with materials supplied through the Red Cross. At the same time living conditions remained overcrowded and insanitary; two bedpans per hut, one razor between twenty men and no toothbrushes, and the food ration still totally insufficient. We depended entirely on the Red Cross parcels to stay above starvation level. Without them no progress whatever in the rehabilitation of the patients could have been made. The days ground along but doctors and patients kept in good heart, aided to no little extent by the padre, who took in the German newspapers and relayed BBC news bulletins from secret receivers in other camps, so that we began to take a fresh interest in the world outside.

On 30 October I was at work in one of the wards when Niebling stamped in, glanced around and, having located me, marched straight in my direction. I braced myself, prepared to receive another of his fault-finding lectures but not for the message he brought. The Chefarzt desired to see me immediately and I was to accompany him forthwith. I knew by now it was futile to ask questions, as Niebling would never have given a straight answer, so I fell in beside him to be quick-marched somewhat apprehensively to the Administration Block.

Möglich was seated at a trestle-table, flipping over a file of papers. Niebling advanced me to the table, halted, clicked his heels and Hitler-saluted. I stood silently to attention, conscious of my heart beat. Möglich looked at the file, looked at me, closed the file – on me I presumed – then without further ado announced,

'Tomorrow morning you will be transferred to Stalag 357.' He looked down, picked up another file and flapped the back of his hand at me in dismissal. Niebling ushered me out.

'Be ready to leave at 0930. That is all. You may return to work.' I meandered back to the lazaret compound pondering on the significance of this turn of events. By great good luck the padre was on one of his visits and was the first person I met to whom I could impart my news. He clapped me on the back.

'The good Lord's looking after you,' he said warmly, 'you're being kicked upstairs. It's a British camp for NCOs. About two miles down the road and a paradise compared with this place.'

'What a relief,' I said, 'I thought I must have somehow blotted my copybook and was maybe off for a spell in the cooler. Why this sudden consideration for my welfare, I wonder?'

'Ah, well you may well ask. They move in a mysterious way their wonders to perform. Never ever give a reason. My advice to you is just to take everything as it comes. Sufficient unto the day. There's nothing you can do about it if you don't like whatever it is, and if it's agreeable thank your lucky stars and enjoy it while it lasts.'

Smith received my news gloomily. 'That means another pair of hands less to keep this show on the road. You may be in luck but I'm certainly not. I hope you don't mind if I lodge an immediate complaint with the bastard. It's intolerable of him to short-staff me on top of everything else.'

But Smith got no change out of Möglich, who told him the order had been received from above, and that was that.

'I didn't believe a word of it,' Smith looked hopping mad. 'He gave me a lot of eye-wash about how sorry he was, and how he would try to obtain a replacement, but I reckon it's all part of his policy to tame us. He thinks the harder we have to work the less time and energy we'll have to give him trouble.'

I worked hard the rest of the day up until lights-out to help Smith get as much done as possible. He was understably despondent but I felt there was nothing I could say to cheer him that might not risk sounding like a eulogy for my own improved prospects. I was really thankful when the morning came and a guard arrived to collect me. I had said my farewells to the patients the previous evening, and now it was hard to say goodbye to colleagues with whom one had shared such experiences as we had, especially to be severing links with the remnants of the Arnhem airborne army.

As the gates of X1 B closed behind me, and I set off down a cobbled lane, my belongings slung in a haversack on my back, my spirits lifted. I had been feeling like a deserter and, irrationally, as if the others regarded me as one. Once outside, on my own, apart from a taciturn and totally uncommunicative guard, in fresh country air, I found myself in an increasingly optimistic frame of mind, looking forward for the first time for many weeks to what might lie ahead. Nothing could be much worse than what lay immediately behind. So be it. Let it lie there.

The new camp lay on top of a hill and was, externally, apart from being smaller and all the uniforms and faces inside the wire British, little different in appearance from the one I had just left. After the usual formalities at the gate I was ushered immediately into the presence of the Camp Commandant. He was elegant and dapper, wearing a faultlessly fitting uniform. Making a slight bow he welcomed me in equally faultless English.

'How do you do. My name is Crawford.'

I must have reacted like countless others to this information because he smiled,

'You no doubt find this surprising?'

When in doubt say nothing. I had no idea what expression my face was registering.

'You wanted to say Crawford doesn't sound German? Nich var?'

Crawford nich var. What is nich var; I was getting really confused with this interview, so continued to hold my tongue but gave him what I hoped was an encouraging amile.

'You would be quite right. I am of Scottish descent.'

I nodded sympathetically. He was lounging nonchalantly against a table and smoking a cigarette in a long holder. He paused to draw on it, exhaling fastidiously through pursed lips.

'I bid you welcome to this camp. I trust you will not find the life too hard. There is, I am afraid, a fuel shortage which is very regrettable, but in other respects I do not think you will find things are too bad.'

He then asked me questions about the circumstances of my capture, and what had since ensued. He asked me to be candid in reply, and I did my best to put in the right sort of word for the prisoners in X1 B, hoping he would not take offence. I could not really tell how he took it. His face wore a fixed drawing-room mien of pleasantry that never altered.

'Well then,' he finally said, indicating the interview was at an end by air-ily waving his arm, 'I need not detain you any longer. So long. So long.'

My guard next escorted me to the hospital compound, a collection of the now-familiar huts, one of which was in use as the Officers' Mess. It was hard to believe such a contrast could have existed between two camps within such a short distance of each other. I was greeted by a mess-corporal who took my baggage and guided me to a room where there were real beds, and led me to tell him which of three empty ones I would prefer. Recalling what the Commandant had said about the fuel shortage I chose the one furthest from the window – I was learning. The corporal then asked if I would like it made up in any special way.

'The orficers orl 'ave their own little fancies Sir,' he said, 'I 'spec you 'ave too. Be pleased to oblige.'

'Thank you corporal.' I was nonplussed at this evidence of refinement. 'Any way will do, as long as it stays tucked up.'

I had a feeling I had disappointed him in some way, but further disap-pointment awaited him.

'Wot, sir!' he exclaimed, as he began to unpack my haversack, 'No perjarmers! 'ave ter get yer some from th'orspittle store. Leave it ter me. Now, Sir, if you'll come this way.'

He led me to the ante-room and introduced me to the President of the Mess, a Scottish padre captured at Dunkirk, who welcomed me in a warm and friendly manner, enquiring how I was off for cigarettes, and in turn introduced me to the other mess members, three doctors, a New Zealand dentist and another padre. I thought I must be dreaming. There were up-to-date medical journals on the table, a well-stocked library with books of every sort, including medical and surgical text-books, a gramophone, armchairs constructed from packing cases, and a sense of security and familiarity of scene not encountered since I had left England. I was, fortuitously, in time for the midday meal. Awaiting us in the dining-room was a large plate of vegetable soup with good potatoes in it, fried Spam, bread, butter and jam and cups of Ovaltine.

'You can't have had much to eat recently,' remarked the mess president, as I wolfed down my portions. I told him about the conditions at X1B.

'I'd heard they were bad but didn't realise they were that bad. They are undoubtedly taking advantage of your inexperience as prisoners.'

'That's what we soon came to realise.'

'Well we won't bother you with any more questions now. Take the afternoon off. Have a rest or a read. We shall all be meeting here again for an evening meal at six-thirty, and you can tell us everything about yourself then.'

I was given a packet of cigarettes and a box of matches and told to make myself comfortable in one of the chairs.

'You can go to bed if you prefer.'

'No. I'll be fine here. Thanks a lot.'

I read and read my way through the medical literature on the table all that afternoon, as starved for mental nourishment as I had been for bodily. I never noticed the passage of time, and was quite unready when the mess-corporal came in and started to empty ash-trays and to tidy up.

'Cook-'ouse very soon nar, sir.'

'You mean it's already time to eat again?'

The corporal looked at me anxiously.

'I'm afride it'll be the sime agin. Cook does 'is best ter mike it temptin. 'Ope it'll soote yer orlrite.'

'Thank you corporal, it will suit me all right.' I said, with convinced and unqualified fervour.

After supper the pipes and cigarettes came out and with them the previously suppressed demand from me for news from home. I told them London was not flattened, poeple were not starving and nothing could stop the Allies winning the war. If Arnhem had succeeded it might very well have been over by now, but Arnhem meant only a temporary set-back.

49

'Glad to hear you say that,' said the mess president. 'We get a news-bulletin from the BBC every day, at about this time, and nothing very exciting or encouraging has come in since then.'

It did not seem proper, although my interest was keenly aroused, to ask exactly how they came by these bulletins; obviously a radio was hidden somewhere in the camp but was not a subject for close public enquiry. So I asked about other things, 'what was the general set-up?'

'Not as good as it has been but not too bad.'

There was a fairly good supply of drugs, dressings and Red Cross parcels – source of the Spam, Ovaltine, cigarettes, tobacco, chocolate, milk and coffee powders that made such a difference to life – also of diet supplement parcels, several hundred in reserve in the hospital; and a good cook in the cook-house who knew how to make things go a long way.

'And what about the Germans, and Crawford? He seemed a decent sort of chap.'

'He's very fair. But don't be deceived by his manner. He can be awk-ward. The guards are mostly quite harmless, in our pay – cigarettes you know. They leave us pretty much to ourselves here in the hospital and even allow us to go for walks outside the camp once a week.'

My new set of colleagues had all been prisoners of war for three or more years, culled from the fall of France or from various operations in the Mediterranean theatre of war, and had all the expedients advanta-geous to life behind barbed-wire well wrapped-up. I found them very heartening. They behaved as if they unquestionably owned the place, and I decided I would be well-content to spend the rest of my captivity with them.

The Senior Medical Officer assigned me to a ward and to a proportion of the morning sick parade, with opportunities to carry out minor treat-ments in a room equipped for the purpose. There I found myself curet-ting warts from the soles of feet, lancing boils and mopping out running ears. None of this was at all exacting and I was by no means kept busy for the whole of the day. At this time I jotted down my recollections of the Battle of Arnhem and of subsequent events to-date, and started a skele-ton diary in an exercise book. I also read medical and surgical text-books, very fast, to refresh my knowledge, and applied myself to the learning of German.

Life was pleasant enough, surprisingly pleasant. The ceremony of the evening BBC news bulletin, received as a typescript and read out by the padre, while the mess corporal kept an eye open for any guards, 'goons', who might be on the prowl, was the focal point of the day. Apart from giving us something positive to look forward to, the fact of being in regular and secret touch with London was in itself a tremendous morale-booster. It allowed us to feel we had the edge on the Germans, as having a more trustworthy source of information than they on the course the war was taking.

I had arrived on a Monday and on the Saturday of that week, 4 November, I was taken for my first walk outside the camp. All of us except the duty officer were able to participate in this welcome excursion, and it was mandatory that we should appear on parade as smartly turned out as possible. Some, who had had their service dresses sent out from England, polished buttons and Sam Brownes, while those of us in battle-dress attended to gaiters and webbing. We set off in an informal body, accompanied by a single guard, down a cobbled country road which wound, at first, through a small forest of fir trees and then open country, to a quite attractive village. There our guard surreptitiously led the way into the local pub by the back door, where we seated ourselves at a well-scrubbed wooden table. This, I was told, was part of the routine. For a few cigarettes the guard was quite willing to trade us a few glasses of beer. It had been put to him at the time, a year or two ago, when the deal was established that, under the Geneva Convention refreshments may be provided for prisoners on a journey. We had naturally agreed never to mention the arrangement. The barmaid, untypically dark and narrow nevertheless served us ungrudgingly and cheerfully, placing glasses of Dunkel Bier, an insipid version of our Mild, before us and refilling them with a nod of her head and a 'bitte schön.'

'Danke shön.' We replied, raising our glasses, 'Sieg heil,' Hail victory – ours of course not yours.

It was a curious situation. There we were, prisoners in the heart of enemy country, having a typically British pub-session and thoroughly enjoying ourselves, all for a couple of packets of cigarettes. I expressed my surprise at this novelty on our way back to the camp. It was nothing. A sufficient number of cigarettes placed in the right hands had been known to purchase the means to escape. But to go as far as that was extremely risky. The difficulty was to be sure which were the right hands, to be sure there would be no betrayal. We were forbidden to accept any kind of present. Some would lure prisoners into giving out large quantities of cigarettes and then take them straight to their senior officer, thereby ingratiating themselves with him. What the officer then did with them was open to question.

Returning to the hospital, rather hungry after the walk, we trooped into the mess. The corporal ushered us in with a complacent gesture towards the table. My eyes followed. On it reposed two crisp, fresh brown, not black, loaves of bread, the civilian variety as the mess president later explained. The mess corporal used to set out for the village of Falingbostel once a week with a suitcase of dirty linen for the laundry. He handed the suitcase over to the laundry women who disappeared into the back of the premises. In the cast amongst the dirty washing were cigarettes. After a short interval she would reappear with the same case, ostensibly packed with last week's now-clean laundry, loaves of fresh bread or other edibles, sausages or the like wrapped within. The guard never suspected, or if he did was too indifferent to interfere. In the event there was always some kind of treat for Saturday evening supper.

All this comparatively good living in stress-free days soon engendered within me a sense of aggressive good health, such as I had not enjoyed since the dark days of Arnhem. With it came a problem; recovery of libido: sudden unbidden primal images of the opposite sex, fantasies of consummation I could have well done without. It was not a subject open to discussion. There was no sex-talk in the mess. No-one wanted their thoughts unnecessarily aroused in that direction. It would only add to the difficulties of living. As doctors we were well aware of the inherent dangers of the appetite in an all-male community growing as it might be fed. It was not a case of St Augustine's 'Lord make me chaste but not just yet'.

It had to be chastity now, for me, never mind anyone else, chastity absolute in every respect. Priggish? No. Severely practical. To reject the conscious thought is to forestall the deed. The unconscious would compensate for the repression. There would be dreams, predictably, where the love-life would express itself, where tensions would be released. Having dealt thus in my mind with this Old Nick I found he troubled me less and less. In fact, although blissfully unaware, I was later to undergo an alteration in circumstances that would make such demands on my reserves of energy as wholly to deplete the fuel of sexuality.

I had spent just over two weeks at Stalag 357 when the bombshell was delivered. I had been perfectly contented, had plenty of professional interests, had accustomed myself to the routine, to the way of life, and made new friends. It was with a feeling akin to panic, therefore, that I received the news from the Senior Medical Officer I was to be ready to leave, with another MO, for an unknown destination in twelve hours.

'Why on earth do they want to move me?' I asked him fretfully, 'I've only just arrived.'

'Can't think. It's as inconvenient for me as it is for you. I need all my MOs. I tried to get Crawford to stop it but it was no use. The order has come from Berlin and he hasn't the authority to countermand it nor, would I guess, the temerity to ring up and question the whys and wherefores.'

Sadly we packed our bags. I was presented with a medical textbook and German grammar, together with a short, but thick French soldier's overcoat. The camp tailor fashioned me some captain's pips for the epaulettes, and attached a Red Cross arm-band to the sleeve. It did not fit too well but I was more than grateful as it kept out the cold and damp, the weather now having apparently settled down permanently for the winter. The guard came to get us just as it was getting dark, and in the dreary atmosphere of a fine cold drizzle we set off at a brisk pace away from that, to me, haven of refuge, towards where? The station perhaps?

Half an hour later the lighted watch-towers of a large wire-ringed camp hove into view. I felt a dreadful premonition.

'My God,' I hissed to the other MO, 'I believe that's X1 B. Don't tell me we're bound for that hell-hole.'

The premonition quickly became a certainty.

'We bloody well are.' The same board was still on the gate.

M.STAMLAGER X1 B
FALINGBOSTEL

The unlocking and locking ceremony at the double gates, the plod in the miserable drizzle to the administration block was a sorry progress downwards into something approaching despair. I found myself once again before Möglich. Niebling had met us and, detailing the guard to remain with the other MO in the ante-room, ushered me in. Left-right, left-right, halt, salute. I was wearing my red beret, the same one I had brought from England and worn ever since discarding the battle-helmet after Arnhem. At-ease. Möglich looked me up and down, as disinterestedly as on the previous occasion I had been before him, then delivered himself of a few brief, toneless sentences. I caught the gist, better at the language even after three weeks' study, but Niebling, as usual, translated.

'The Chefarzt bids you welcome for the night.' My heart gave a leap. 'Early tomorrow you will be proceeding to Saxony.'

'Oh, thank you, thank you,' I effused. The relief was unspeakable. Anywhere was better than here.

'That is all.'

I retired a step, saluted again, and marched briskly to the door, anxious to escape from Möglich's presence before he might undergo a change of mind. I sat in the ante-room while the other MO went in. Together again after a short interval I looked at him with raised eyebrows.

'Somewhere in Thuringia, tomorrow early,' he responded.

'Where's that?'

'God knows. Somewhere in the middle of the country I think. I'm for Saxony. Good old ancestral territory. Wherever we go we'll be well out of this place, I can tell you.' Niebling had materialised, unnoticed by us, and overheard my last remark. He looked none too pleased.

'Come,' he ordered coldly, 'your friends in the lazaret are expecting you.'

We traversed the old familiar mud paths to the lazaret compound. The nights were drawing in and the huts were already locked, and shuttered to exclude the lights inside. Blackout regulations were as strict as at home. Somewhere to the west searchlights were flinging a meaningless pattern of moving white blobs on the underside of the low clouds. Niebling unlocked the door, and once again I was back with the smell of the unwashed and infected, not as strong as when I had left, but nauseating enough after the aseptic atmosphere of Stalag 357.

'Hello, Pip, Ian, everybody. Hope you're all OK.' I introduced the other MO, and we were introduced in turn to a Colonel in the Australian Medical Corps, who had fetched up at X1 B in my absence and was also bound for Thuringia in the morning.

Pip Smith could not resist a rueful smile and an envious comment

'It's not as bad as it was but we're all heartily sick of it. You lucky so and sos.'

'Maybe,' I said, 'you never know. Out of the frying pan and all that.'

I thought it would only rub salt into his wounds to regale him with the favourable conditions I had recently been enjoying. Short of rebuilding the place and changing all the people in charge there was nothing much he could really do to improve the living conditions. It was a correction camp and, apparently to some extent, a transit camp, and that was all there was to it. I did, however, encourage him to continue in his fight for the prisoners' rights, not that he really would ever have let up, detailing some of the wrinkles I had learned from the veteran prisoners.

'They told me things were equally rough at first but, in their experience, got better in so far as they kept on and on at the Germans about the Convention.'

I also passed on the latest BBC news from the night before. Little military progress, but plenty of destruction of the Reich from the air. Berlin bombed again, railways and factories taken out.

'There won't be a winter offensive' commented Smith drily, 'tanks need firm going, and plenty of daylight for maximum progress with full air support. As I see it we'll be sweating it out here all winter, with supplies becoming more and more difficult as the RAF chew up the communications and stores.'

'But,' I said, feeling it incumbent upon me to say something cheerful, 'when we get across the Rhine the Hanover Plain'll be the spearhead break-out ground as intended after Arnhem. This camp'll be in direct line for early liberation.'

'*When* we get across the Rhine.'

I would not have changed places with Smith and his remaining band of officers for all the tea in China, and could sense that they would have given much to be going my way, to whatever it might be leading. The conversation became desultory and soon we turned in. I was very glad to be able to supplement the meagre bedding with my French overcoat, for the room grew dank and cold as the stove died.

We were called at 0400 hours the next morning, extracted from the sleeping hut like three sardines from a tin, to the annoyance of the others who grumbled at the noise, as we were obliged, perforce, to clump about gathering ourselves together; down the corridor to the ablutions by the light of the guard's lantern, back to the bunk to finish our packing, then after brief goodbyes out into the yet very dark night. It had stopped raining and the sky had cleared. A few stars were showing and it was very cold. First stop the Abwer, security block, to be searched. It was more thorough than that which we underwent on our first arrival. But they did not think to examine the thin end of my tie, within the lining of which reposed the fingernail-sized compass I had brought out from England, nor to unroll the sleeves of my shirt, in the folds of one of which was concealed my printed mini-map of Western Europe. Nor did they examine closely the German grammar. A flip through the pages, an expression of approval and it was handed back – in the thick brown-paper dust cover with which I had invested it. If they had removed the cover they would have discovered the few, thin, closely-written pages of my telegraphic diary torn from the exercise-book, which itself aroused no comment as it now only contained notes I had made from the German grammar. We were all three cleared and, once again, stood before the entrance gates, the searchlights on the twin towers stabbing the road to Falingbostel down which we were soon marching.

IV

Journey
(16–20 November 1944)

We had two guards; a corporal for the Australian colonel and other MO, and a private for myself. He was very youthful-looking, still in his teens, slightly built, with thick-lens glasses and a bad stammer. I think he too was glad to be out of the camp, glad of a change from that dreary place, for he jabbered cheerfully to the corporal all the way down the road. The metal half-moons on the heels of our boots rang on the cobbles, and we swung along at a good pace behind the corporal and his lantern.

For a wild moment I thought of escape. We were now back in the wooded area we had passed through on the day of our arrival, and a quick dash into the deeper darkness of the trees,before the guards could unsling and aim their rifles, seemed to hold out a tempting prospect of almost certain success. But what then? The alarm bell would soon ring in the camp, and in no time the area would be crawling with armed Germans and their Alsatian dogs. No thank you. Not just now. At Stalag 357 they had drilled it into me that any escape from the heart of Germany, to be successful, had to be faultlessly organised in terms of civilian clothes and identity papers, water-tight cover story, train time-tables known to the minute, much more than a smattering of German, and preferably a companion to share the burdens of endless watchfulness, split-second decisions and constant anxiety.

At length we arrived at the station and joined a crowd of foot-stamping, body-slapping, breath-frosted Germans of both sexes waiting on the platform. Scarcely a glance was thrown in our direction, all eyes being turned towards an approaching train, discernible by a distant display of sparks from the engine's funnel. As it drew to a halt there was a stampede for the doors and a most unmannerly use of male German elbows in order to achieve the prize of a seat. The lack of courtesy shown to the opposite sex would no doubt have been gratifying to a modern woman's liberation movement, but it seemed to me a dismal contrast to the social custom then prevailing at home. In fact, when the train got on the move again, it was apparent that the majority of those standing in the corridors and compartments were women. As prisoners we were spared the unseemly scramble. Our corporal merely gave an order and the crowd parted like the red sea, leaving us a space to stand, but not apart, which was just as well. There was no heating on the train we were all jammed so tightly together we engendered our own. There we stood, packed round with German ladies of various ages who conversed together animatedly and good-humouredly; such sociability in such circumstances at this hour of the morning made yet another strong contrast to the travelling habits of home.

After going for a while with stops at several stations, the compartment cleared sufficiently for enough slatted wooden seats to become vacant for our party to sit down. We were travelling third class. I said to the Aussie colonel,

'You know, as officer prisoners we should be travelling first. Convention says so. German prisoner officers are always accorded that comfort at home, and these seats are exceedingly hard and uncomfortable. At least I find them so.'

'Too bloody right they are. I'll see what the corporal has to say about it.' He turned to the guard sitting next to him, morosely clasping his rifle between his knees. The colonel had been in the country long enough to have acquired 'prisoners', 'kreegy' German.

'Ich bin offizier; nich var? Warum nicht fahren erste klasse?'

'Ho. Ho!' The corporal suddenly came to life, galvanised by mirth.

'Das ist ein good vun.' His English was passable pidgeon.

'Ho. Ho! Erste klasse?. You no see erste klasse on dese zugs. Dese zugs immer der same.' He patted the seat. 'Erste klasse nur for generals and führers, Ho. Ho. Ho!'

'Ho.Ho. Bloody funny,' said the colonel. 'Tell us where we're going then. Wohin fahren uns?'

'Nach Magdeburg. Then you and you, he pointed to the colonel and the other MO, 'vill mit mich kommen. Und you,' he pointed at me, 'vill mit ihn gehen.' he nodded at the other guard.

So we were to be split up at Magdeburg. I tried to remember where it was; so many maps of Germany in so many newspapers since the war began showing where the RAF had struck its nightly blows. Somewhere on the line between Hanover and Berlin? It crossed my mind that I might ask to visit the washroom and steal a surreptitious glance at my minimap, but it hardly seemed worth it. Magdeburg was not to be the ultimate destination, and we should no doubt know where we were soon enough when we reached our journey's end.

The train grumbled on. We had been provided with cheese sand-wiches for the journey, soon demolished, and had passed most of the time dozing fitfully on the hard seats. At four in the afternoon, stiff and bored, I said, trying to enliven the tedium,

'What I would really like now is a nice cup of tea. Perhaps they'll give us one at Magdeburg.'

At which the corporal suddenly stood up.

'Here ist Magdeburg.'

I looked out of the window. We were passing slowly through gloomy suburbs; gaunt, shattered, dusty buildings showed ample evidence of the destructive activities of the Royal Air Force, but the station when we reached it seemed to be intact, working to full capacity. Platforms were crowded, trains coming and going and, if it ever had been a prime target, the Germans' ability to make rapid and effective repairs must have been sadly underestimated. As I saw it everything looked to be functioning smoothly and normally.

The guards shepherded us into a spacious, well-lit, impeccably clean subway to an arrival and departure train indicator, at which they stopped and began to argue loudly between themselves, while I looked with interest at the busy stream of people thronging by, searching their faces for signs of exhaustion or distress. They were supposed to be at the end of their tether, oppressed with the knowledge of having lost the war, war-weary and disillusioned, semi-starving and apathetic. If so they gave no public indication of any such thing. The whole impression I gained was of a well-organised, intense and purposeful efficiency. Soldiers in transit were moving about everywhere, lean, tough-looking and smartly turned out. I saw several high-ranking officers, a naval captain, a general and a Luftwaffe chief, all accorded the greatest respect by the other ranks who made way for and saluted them promptly. I pondered the paradox: did they know in reality they had their backs to the wall? If so there was not much difference between their bearing now and ours after Dunkirk, or were they so conditioned to the expectation of victory by their own propaganda as to be aggressively living in a fool's paradise? Either way,

I thought, if this is a typical cross-section of the German public there is a hard slog ahead for the Allied armies, they are far from finished yet. The women wore drab-coloured clothes but nowhere was there evidence of real poverty. The children were warmly clad and well-nourished. One young girl of about sixteen or seventeen, dressed in skiing costume, came up to our guards and asked them, I gathered from her gestures, to mind her skis while she went to collect her 'gepack'. Soon she returned with a large rucksack, reclaimed and shouldered her skis, and went off with a gay wave of her hand. Germans apparently still took holidays.

At last the guards finally decided on the trains we should be taking, and the corporal announced the party would now split up. I was bound for Leipzig in an hour's time, the colonel and other MO for Nordhausen half an hour later.

'There's time enough for tea then.' I half facetiously returned to my earlier refrain. 'We're entitled to refreshments on a journey. Worth trying it on Colonel?

'OK. No harm in trying.' He turned to the corporal,

'Kernen wir em cupper tea haben? Wir sint durstig.'

'Tasse Tee? Ho. Ho!' The corporal was off again in fits.

'No Tee in Magdeburg. Kein Tee in whole damn Reich.' He paused, stopped shaking, looked at his watch, 'aber vielleicht some Kaffee.'

'Danke schön,' said the colonel, adding as an aside to us, 'It'll be better than nothing filthy though it is.'

The corporal despatched the little guard to discover the whereabouts, if any, of a refreshment room, and soon he came back with the welcome news there was a Red Cross canteen on one of the platforms where we might be served. Trotting happily ahead, as pleased with the prospect no doubt as we were, he took us to a side-door of the canteen where a girl handed out hot soup, solid with barley, and then treated us to cups of ersatz coffee. We offered to pay but the girl smilingly declined our proffered marks. All officer prisoners were supposed to receive a standard regular payment from the German government for the purpose of buying such articles as soap and shaving materials from the prison canteens. I had been given sixty marks on leaving X1 B, the only payment I ever received from them, but there was never any difficulty in acquiring marks on the black market as long as one had cigarettes with which to trade.

We parted company with mutual expressions of 'good luck' and 'a safe journey home' – and I was on my own, for the first time. No support now from anyone of my own ilk or rank. Nevertheless not unsupported. I was a believer in the existence of a personal power beyond ourselves to help us when in need, specifically as formulated in the tenets of the

Christian Faith, the fruit of instruction at school, and pretty well stuck at that intellectual level. I was not so naive as to imagine confession of this faith would insulate me from pain, suffering or other ordeals, but that, whatever might come, there was a source of strength available on sincere application to enable me to meet it.

The little guard herded me to the platform where our train, a far more imposing assembly than the last one, stood wreathing the legs of boarding passengers in thin clouds of steam vented, I hoped, from a heating system. He prodded me into the corner seat of an empty compartment, which he did his best to reserve to ourselves by shouting, 'dienst Abteil', duty compartment , and 'Englische Kriegsgefanghene', pointing at me, whenever anybody else tried to enter. This worked well at Magdeburg, and he winked at me and talked away to himself after each success. But at the next station where we stopped a whole horde of young girls, Hitler Youth or Land Army, something like that, descended upon the train, swept him aside, swamping the compartment and squeezing us into our corner with giggles and shrill laughter. They stared at me, pointing and whispering behind their hands to each other, then turned their attention upon my guard. He looked outraged and indignant and yet was so young the effect was ludicrous. The girls ragged him unmercifully, pointing derisively at the large cherry-wood Tyrolean type pipe which he smoked in rapid puffs while his face became redder and redder. Eventually he abandoned his pose of offended representative of the Wehrmacht and pulled one of the girls' pigtails. This led to screams and howls and a general assault upon his person. One girl pulled his cap down over his eyes, another tried to pull off his boots, another snatched at his pipe, while he swung his arms like windmills and tried to fend them off. I squeezed further into my corner and tried to dissociate myself from the scene, aware that it was really all in fun but beginning to wonder how far it might go before I became embroiled. Suddenly the turmoil ceased. The guard got his pipe back, straightened his hat and launched into a patter of what must have been funny stories, as everything he said was greeted by howls of mirth from the girls. Then, after a little while, they all settled down and the mood completely changed. One of the girls started singing and, quite spontaneously, all the others joined in, taking parts and harmonising in true clear voices. I did not know the songs; they may have been patriotic, political, directed perhaps against my country, but whatever their content they were good to listen to. The effect for me, in the dim light, with a feeling of isolation in space as the train sped through the unfamiliar country, was unexpectedly moving. They sang with an easy expertise, as a Welsh choir might sing hymns.

61

A few stations further on the girls all got out and we once again had the compartment to ourselves.

The guard and I both dozed, unable to communicate except at a very basic level of mixed German and English monosyllables, supplemented by somewhat fatuous mime. In any case it was all the time getting darker and the train was unlit. By the time we arrived at Leipzig it was entirely dark, the sky was clear and all the stars brilliantly ashine. Searchlights were weaving about in the distance and I hoped this was not to be one of the nights chosen by the RAF for another attack on the station, reputedly one of the largest in Germany and already the scene of much previous attention. It resembled, in lay-out, a larger edition of Waterloo in London. A spray of platforms leading from a broad general concourse behind which had stood ticket-offices, left-luggage rooms, bars, restaurants and administrative offices, now reduced to huge piles of shapeless concrete and a melee of rubble, while above, where the roof had once been, was a gaping void open to the stars.

My guard led me into the equivalent of a Railway Transport Officer's office and stood me against a wall.

'Blieben sie hier.'

I nodded my assent, and he moved over to join a crowd of soldiers at the RTO's table, to find out, I presumed, where we were to go next and I waited, self-consciously, as a swarm of armed men pushed and shouldered past me. Some stared in an unmistakably hostile manner at my Red Beret, but seemed to lose interest when they noticed the Red Cross arm-band. The majority never so much as glanced in my direction, too busy finding out about their own trains to waste time on a foreigner. If I had but known it then an apparently unescorted prisoner-of-war was a common sight in Leipzig, where at least sixty-per-cent of the population were war-imported non-Germans,

My guard rejoined me in an obvious hurry and grabbed me by the arm.

'Komm. Schnell.'

We ran at the double to a platform at the other end of the concourse and boarded another train, already full of German soldiers in Pullman-type coaches. The guard managed to find us seats, hard wooden slats as before, and I subsided wearily, thankful not to be having to stand. The atmosphere in the crowded carriage seemed unusually subdued, even my normally chatty guard was silent, and then I noticed all the soldiers bore signs of having been wounded. This train was fitted with black-out blinds and provided with dim lighting, enough for me to take in the scene with interest. Once the train got under way the soldiers began to stir themselves. Perhaps they felt as I did about the RAF, a moving train in darkened country being safer and, therfore, preferable than one stuck in a large potential target station. One of them produced a mouth-organ and they all started to sing, a mixture of songs, the vigorous and the plaintive, the boisterous and, I expect, the bawdy. One tune and the first line of it somehow lodged in my head, 'Ein kleine Lied soll uns verbinden'. The sentiment was easy to understand, the universal sentiment of war-parted lovers. Our song, our link. No doubt they had their own Forces' Sweetheart, their own Vera Lynn to sing for them 'We'll meet again'. Ah, but, I asked myself, are they singing to keep up their spirits or is their morale really high? Some were without arms or legs and could be giving expression to pleasure at being out of the line – for good, and who would blame them? Perhaps the truth was simpler and I was foolish to look for motive. Probably they were singing neither to sustain themselves nor to celebrate, but because they were soldiers; and soldiers given half a chance, wherever they are, like to sing.

Three-quarters of an hour later we stopped at a station where my guard indicated we were to leave the train. We had been travelling eighteen hours and I wondered for how much longer it was to go on. The starlit night permitted a fair degree of visibility, and I could see the station was deserted.

'Wo sind uns?' I hazarded in my monosyllabic German.

'Oschatz.' replied the guard. 'Komm.'

We headed for a sign marked 'Ausfahrt' where there was a gate chained and padlocked. Beside it a glimmer of light showed beneath the door of an office. My guard knocked on the door and, after a short pause, a uniformed official appeared struggling into his tunic. My guard presented his credentials and mine.

'Englische Kriegsgefangene fur Stalag Vier G.'

The official looked carefully at the papers, looked me up and down, took keys from his pocket, unlocked the gate and, after issuing some directions, waved us on.

'Gute Nacht. Heil Hitler.'

My guard shot out his right arm and clicked his heels, 'Heil Hitler.'

We found ourselves in a small town, through the streets of which we marched for some twenty minutes, our footsteps sounding unnaturally loud, until we came to what looked like a small factory. Here a sentry challenged us and, after the usual thorough formalities took us inside and handed us over to a duty orderly who, in turn, led us along a corridor to an office out of which opened two other doors. The orderly knocked on one of them. Nothing happened. He knocked again, louder this time, and shortly the door was flung open and a rotund, short-sighted, angry-looking man emerged in his socks and braces, rubbing his eyes and yawning.

'Was ist das?'

'Entschuldigen sie bitte, Herr Hauptmann, der Englische Kriegsgefangene.'

'Ach so.' The captain turned to me. 'Your name please.'

His accent was good. I told him what he asked.

'I have been expecting you. Tonight you sleep here. Tomorrow in the morning we talk.'

'Thank you Herr Hauptmann.'

He returned to his room and the orderly took us along the corridor to another where there were two beds.

'Toilette. Waschraum?' I said anxiously. The soup and coffee imbibed at Magdeburg were by now exerting an intolerable pressure. The orderly looked at me suspiciously, eyeing my haversack which I retained hold of, hoping if possible for a chance to clean my teeth, but he beckoned me to follow and took me to a small place where I could perform the necessary, all the while standing in the doorway, at ease, watching me. I was obviously thought to be not without an intention to escape if I could.

When I returned to the bedroom my little guard, having merely removed his jackboots and tunic, was already flat on his back, asleep and snoring. I was not long in divesting myself of boots, trousers, battle-dress, blouse and gaiters getting between the blankets and drifting off to sleep, my last thoughts being taken up with the absurd question of how it was the guard had had no apparent need to relieve himself before going to bed whereas I had been bursting. Perhaps he had found somewhere while I was waiting for him in the RTO's office at Leipzig, as that was the only time he had not had me in constant sight, and vice versa, since Magdeburg.

I was aroused by the noise of his jackboots banging on the wooden floor. He was opening the window-shutters. He then proceeded to fold his blankets and to flap about as if about to undergo a kit inspection. I sat up.

'Guten Morgen,' he said pleasantly, 'you have good schlept?'

'Very good danke schön.' I could have done with several hours more.

'Now aufstehen.'

'Aufstehen? Already?'

'Oh ja. Schnell. Schnell.'

'Always bloody schnell,' I grumbled at him, 'warum immer schnell? Warum nicht take your time, or there's no hurry, or breakfast won't be for half an hour ...'

'Bitte? Was haben sie gesagt? Ich verstehe nicht.'

'Oh never mind. Nothing. Nichts.' I remembered I was to have an interview with the Hauptmann and indicated by a rehearsal of the motions that I wished to wash, shave, clean my teeth, in short again visit the washroom. The guard's face lightened.

'OK, das Ich verstehe. Komm.'

He led me back down the passage and I availed myself freely of the facilities, which were very good. I had felt decidedly rumpled after the journey and meant to spruce up for the Hauptmann.We were of equal rank and I did not want to put him in the advantageous position of being able to criticise my turn-out. I even succeeded by dint of further play-acting to obtain from my guard the wherewithall to polish my boots. I was taking all this at a leisurely pace and he kept looking at his watch. When I had finished I said again hopefully,

'Now breakfast? Früstück?' He shook his head.

'Spater. Erste der Hauptmann!'

The Hauptmann, who the night before had looked dishevelled and much put out, was now well-groomed and affable, seated behind his desk with a cup of coffee at his elbow, and exuding a strong smell of Eau-de-Cologne.

'Take a seat, captain.' He proffered me a vacant chair.

'Thank you.'

'Will you join me in a coffee?'

'Thank you.'

'You have had a long journey. I trust you were well looked after?' he looked meaningfully at my guard, 'and had a good night's rest?'

I had come to feel really quite attached to the little guard and was anxious that he should come out of his assignmant to my person with some credit. 'Thank you. I assure you I have been treated most considerately, and with absolute correctness throughout. The 'consideration' I did not expect to earn him many marks, but 'correctness' was all-important. He should get a bonus for that.

'That is good. You are now in the headquarters of Stalag Four Gee. At ten o'clock you will be interviewed by the Chefarzt of the Stalag, who will assign you to your medical duties. Meanwhile, until then, you will be in the company of the Senior British Padre, whom I have asked to see that you get some breakfast.' On which cheerful note he rang a small hand bell and summonsed a clerical orderly. There was a rapid exchange of German between them that I could not follow, at the end of which my guard was dismissed and had made his exit before I could say a word of thanks or farewell. I assumed he would be returning to Falingbost poor little devil. The Hauptmann rose. I did likewise. He walked round the desk and escorted me to the door.

'The orderly will show you where to go now.'

'May I collect my things from the bedroom?'

'Of course. Auf wiedersehen.'

The Senior British Padre to the Stalag occupied a small box-like cabin adjoining a large hut inhabited by French prisoners, into which I was first taken. The orderly said something in German to one of the Frenchmen who advanced toward me with outstretched hand.

'Bonjour mon capitaine.'

I took it. 'Bonjour monsieur.' I had enough command of the French language to be able to carry on a reasonable conversation and quickly understood I was to be their guest until the padre returned from one of his pastoral duties, an early service elsewhere in the camp. The French pumped me for news, at the same time making me comfortable in a packing-case armchair with a cup of excellent coffee and a cigarette. They were very friendly and I warmed to them. Although all had been prisoners since the fall of France, they were from the Services, and not expatriated civilians as I understood had been those at Falingbostel and, it would seem, had not suffered such severe conditions. They were relaxed and urbane and enthusiastic for the Allies, especially for the liberation of Paris, spearheaded by one of their own Free French units. They commiserated with me over the Arnhem debacle and complimented me on my good fortune at still being alive and well. 'The war will soon be over. You will not have to stay here long,' they said, 'but we are beginning to get worried in case the Russians get here before the Allies.' I thought to myself, but did not say so, the word 'Allies' was supposed to include the Russians. But it was not the case in this part of the world, apparently, and it was to become even more apparent as time went by, the Russians were regarded as something quite independant and otherwise, a menacing force, despite the 'brotherhood in arms against the common enemy', that did not subscribe to the accepted European rules of the war game. They were a force which the general run of prisoners would not choose as liberators if there was a choice, especially the Russian prisoners who knew themselves to be already disowned by Stalin, and in mortal fear of reprisal. The fact was that all, except possibly dedicated communists, were hoping and praying that deliverance would come from the West.

The padre was a genial host who gave me a breakfast of fried spam in his room while once again exposing me to the ever-insatiable prisoner of war appetite for outside news. I went through my, by now, stereotyped rigmarole between mouthfuls and then, over yet another cup of coffee, I in my turn pressed him for information about Stalag IV G. Oschatz, he confirmed, was the headquarters of the stalag, actively concerned in the administration of the whole sector. The stalag sector itself was spread over several hundred square miles of Saxony, and the prisoners, being all under the rank of corporal, were employed by the Germans in work of one sort or another theoretically not supposed to be of military advantage to themselves. To effect this, prisoners were split up into working commandos, small groups of between twenty-five to one hundred and fifty men, housed in huts built for the purpose or other convenient buildings, such as commandeered cafés, near their site of work. There were several sub-areas in the stalag sector, corresponding to density of commandos; at Leipzig, for example, where some two thousand British prisoners were employed, and other subareas at Vurzen, Badlausig and Grimma. Each subarea had a medical officer who 'practised' among the prisoners of his own nationality. The Stalag was of mixed nationality, preponderantly French, with British and Russians in about equal proportions, and a sprinkling of Dutch, Americans and Danes. Each sub-area had a German doctor who controlled the prisoner doctors, and at Oschatz resided the Chefarzt, head doctor of the stalag, by whom I was shortly to be interviewed.

The administrative staff of British prisoners at Oschatz was headed by the Chief Man-of-Confidence, elected by the prisoners to represent them and handle their interests with the Gennans. This involved him in maintaining contact with the Red Cross organisation headquarters at Geneva, and in contriving to ensure that each prisoner received his just quota of Red Cross parcels, clothes, books and other benefits received from that organisation by the camp. The prisoners' mail for the whole stalag also passed through Oschatz, and the Man-of-Confidence had about fourteen British on the administrative staff to assist in dealing with these matters. The padre, stationed at Oschatz visited the subareas in turn, and was therefore an important link-man through whom the commandos could be kept in the overall picture, and be made to feel themselves in close touch with headquarters and the main stream of events.

'You're sure to be sent to one of the sub-areas,' he told me, 'where you'll have considerable liberty to travel about visiting the sick in their commando billets and, consequently, will lead a life of some interest and variety, as I do. This is not a bad stalag as stalags go, and Red Cross parcels are in good supply.

'These parcels seem to be the be all and end all of camp life,' I commented, 'certainly of the ones I have seen so far.'

'They most certainly are. Prisoners' lives revolve around them. The Man-of-Confidence has an unenviable task in seeing that the individual issues are fair and square and above board. Any hint of inequity and he would be in deep trouble. You will find that prisoner-of-war life generates many tensions. Prisoners can become moody, sullen, suspicious, jealous of their meagre possessions, and not averse to kicking up a rumpus, even over trivial matters, if they feel the need to release their tension or divert their boredom. On the whole they cope remarkably well with their circumstances, and keep cheerful and good tempered. It is part of my job to help them stay that way, and it will be yours too. You must never compromise your profession's reputation for discretion and impartiality. They will need to feel they can always safely confide in you, with privacy, at any time. Have you had any training in psychology?'

'You mean trick-cycling? Afraid not. There was no room for that on the curriculum when I was a medical student.'

'Pity. Nor have I. Human behaviour takes a lot of understanding and some human behaviour in the camps especially so.' He glanced at his watch. 'Time coming up for your interview. I'll return you to the Hauptmann.'

The Hauptmann took me over, led me along winding corridors and up a staircase, and ushered me into the august presence of the Chefarzt. He was an elderly balding man with a weary look on his face, and what he had to say to me, translated by the Hauptmann was brief and to the point.

'I see that you have not been a prisoner for very long and I shall therefore send you to Naunhof, where you will only have to look after about eight hundred prisoners. I always try to treat prisoners fairly and if you co-operate with me I will co-operate with you. You will find prisoners constantly try to avoid work by reporting sick with trivialities. You must be severe with such men. You will be supervised by the German over-doctor in your area, and if you are not considered satisfactory you will be removed and sent to an Oflag where you will forgo the privilege of practising your profession. You may take walks without a guard within a prescribed area but if you try to escape you will, after your inevitable recapture, be sent to a punishment camp, the other British doctors in the stalag will have their freedom of movement cancelled and the British medical services to your own men will curtailed. You understand?'

'Yes, Herr Oberstabsarzt.' I understood very well. He was exerting moral pressure on me not to try to escape because if I did my medical colleagues and their prisoner patients would suffer in consequence.

'That is all then. Good day.'

Two thoughts were uppermost in my mind as the Hauptmann escorted me back to his office. I had not been asked to give an undertaking 'on my honour' not to escape and was therefore at liberty to do so, if so minded, and the Chefarzt had taken it for granted I would prefer to serve the prisoners in the professional capacity he had indicated, and had presumably laid down the same conditions for the other doctors in the sector. It was a case of Hobson's choice. Not an unreasonable way to exert leverage on a doctor. Not an unreasonable man? It was my one and only meeting with him, but I had found out his own claim to fair trearment for the prisoners was borne out by the men themselves who nearly all spoke well of him. He did not bear comparison with Möglich at X1 B. I discovered he had himself been a prisoner of war in England during the First World War so that a genuine concern for prisoner's welfare would not be out of character. I was extremely glad to find I was not going to be shut up behind barbed wire again. I could not yet imagine exactly what my way of life was to be like; but to be able to take walks unescorted – there was something hitherto quite unexpected.

The day was Saturday, I was due to leave for Naunhof on the Monday and I spent the weekend billeted with a French doctor also bound for Naunhof. He was middle-aged, rather portly, and immensely good company. He wore a small tooth-brush moustache, cut so short that only its severely regulated shape prevented one from assuming he had simply neglected to shave properly. We conversed in French as he had little or no English. I asked him, with suitable apologies for the personal nature of the question, why he clipped his moustache so short instead of letting it grow to a more usual length.

'Ah,' he replied with a twinkle in his eye, 'ça pique les femmes.' I understood that to mean 'stimulates the ladies'.

'But what ladies?' I pursued the topic with interest. 'Surely there are no ladies around here?'

'Ah, my friend, that would be telling. But believe me they very much appreciate the feel of it.' He smiled significantly at me and caressed his upper lips from side to side with his right forefinger, which he then laid against the side of his nose, and gave a prodigious wink.

In the afternoon I watched a football match played between two teams of British prisoners. They had somehow obtained the regulation kit, shorts, striped shirts and knee-length stockings, and the game was conducted in a professional manner with referee and linesmen, refreshments at half-time, marked-out filed goalposts, the lot. But the highlight of my stay at Oschatz was being taken by the French doctor to a revue given by French prisoners early on the Sunday evening. This was an astonishing performance of comic turns, risky as the butt of the jokes were the Germans who, if they had known how much the micky was being taken out of them would have been understandably incensed with rage, but the sketches were so cleverly phrased as to give no obvious offence, while the the main audience were left in no doubt for whom the custard pie was intended. Risqué too; the silent antics of the Absent-minded Fisherman and One-armed Flautist brought the house down.

Germans in the audience fell about in heaps, amply compensated for the thinly disguised insults they had unwittingly endured in the other acts. I had not had such a good laugh since leaving England for Arnhem. The evening was rounded off with a few rubbers of Bridge in the French quarters. I partnered the French doctor, who played a cunning hand, and ended up two packets of Gauloises the richer. Altogether a good day.

Early the next morning the French doctor and I were bidden to the Hauptmann's office and introduced to our escort, a lance-corporal, who took us in tow. Our journey to Naunhof involved a return to and change of trains at Leipzig with a wait there of three hours.

'Rather than spend the time waiting about at the station, I have given orders to the Gefreite to take you to visit your medical colleagues at the prisoners' revier.'

'Revier?' I had not yet come across the word. He searched for the right translation.

'Klein Krankenhaus. You might say small infirmary – they will give you refreshments and no doubt be glad of a short change of company. So. Good bye for now. Auf wiedersehen.'

'Auf wiedersehen Herr Hauptmann, und vielin dank.' I now knew the Germans preferred to be addressed in their own language, and I was gradually coming on in it.

During our march to the station at Oschatz I asked the French doctor if he had understood the exchanges between the Hauptmann and myself, as he kept saying he did not speak any English, and did he realise we were stopping off at Leipzig.

'Mais oui, bien sur. Anglais? J'en comprend assez mais Je ne le parle pas.' Then he muttered on to himself almost too fast for me to follow, 'les sales Bosches, the bloody Germans, been moving me backwards and forwards all over the stalag for years. They never keep you very long in one place.'

I was now accustomed to the novelty of rail travel in enemy country and began to pay closer attention to the formalities at the barriers. Examination was unhurried and very thorough. The gefreite's own pass, Ausweis, was closely scrutinised, and then the papers photographs relating to ourselves with frequent glances in our direction. Some of the civilians, perhaps with season-tickets and obviously well-known to the railway official, went through on the nod, but others were held back for a very close inspection and it was obvious, as I had earlier been warned, that to escape by train would require complete familiarity with railway bureaucratic procedures, and total knowledge of the documentation necessary in order to proceed unchallenged.

Leipzig station looked even more knocked about in daylight than it had. in the dark, and in the course of the half-hour's walk from it to the revier I saw further widespread evidence of the destructive capacity of the RAF's night raids.But the roads were clear, trams and traffic moved freely and numerous people were going about their business, maybe bloodied but manifestly unbowed. Everything I had seen so far had testified to the resilience and toughness of the German nation. They had been ferocious opponents at Arnhem and were still going to be no push-over, utterly hopeless though their military position might appear on paper, squeezed relentlessly between east and west. Hitler's stature seemed undiminished, especially since the abortive attempt on his life and he had promised them victory through the deployment of new secret weapon. I had at one time been on the receiving end of both the V1, flying bombs, and V2, rockets. Had they anything else up their sleeve? The French and British at Oschatz thought not. I wondered.

The revier was a grim-looking building, one of a row of unassuming three-storey tenement houses in Gneisenau Strasse. It had once been a youth hostel, now it served as a minor hospital, with limited facilities for the sick of three nations, British, French and Russian. The British and French doctors shared living quarters, with their medical orderlies, on the top floor. The Russians were isolated in the basement. The interior was gloomy in the extreme, with stone walls unrelieved by paint or wall-paper, plain wooden floors, sparse furniture and naked electric light bulbs. We were taken up to the living quarters, where soon we were joined by the doctors who had been taking a sick-parade in a large room on the ground floor. They looked exhausted, grey with fatigue, but brightened when they saw us.

'Hallo, good to see you,' the British captain advanced upon me, 'I'm Webster and this is Médecin Capitaine Henri Denis.'

We shook hands all round.

'Do take a seat. Cigarette?'

We all subsided onto wooden, kitchen-style chairs grouped round a plain table. The two French doctors knew each other well and were soon deep in conversation. Webster told me he had been in the Leipzig revier for more than a year and was heartily sick of it. The work was grinding, and numerous air-raid alerts cut into the night's sleep. He said he envied me my posting to Naunhof, a relatively quiet and pleasant country town, and by the time he had finished regaling me with the details of his life I was very glad to be going where I was and getting well away from this city. I did my best to raise his spirits with optimistic forecasts about the war as it had looked from the other, English side of the channel. We shared a meal with them, and when the time came for us to leave they insisted on accompanying us to the station. At Webster's instigation we boarded a tram, he produced the money to purchase our fares and rattled away in German to the female ticket collector. I commented on his facility with the language.

'Take my advice,' he said earnestly, 'learn this bloody lingo as quickly as possible. If ever you get sent here ...,' 'Which heaven forbid,' I muttered, 'you'll have to travel all over the city visiting the commandos who are too sick to come to the revier, and you'll need to argue with the Germans in German. Life's one hell of a long argument with them all the time.'

With promises to come and visit them again if it could be contrived, we said our good-byes as we boarded the train at Leipzig station, and at length arrived at Naunhof at half-past-two in the afternoon, on Monday 20 November.

V

Naunhof
(20 November – 14 December)

Naunhof turned out to be a small country town, albeit boasting a Rathaus (Town Hall) and Platz (Town Square), with a residential area nearer the station of large villas occupied by wealthy business, professional or party men who commuted to Leipzig daily. There were three factories on the outskirts, one for the processing of rabbit skins, and the other two, reputedly, for the manufacture of some parts of the Messerschmitt fighter aeroplane.

It lay eleven miles or so to the south-east of Leipzig, on one of the lines to Dresden, with the notorious Colditz a mere fifteen miles away, again to the south-east. The surrounding country was typical of the plain of Saxony, gently undulating, wooded, with long, wide views of open farmland from the higher ground. Leipzig was easily visible on a clear day. The open land was all under intense cultivation, supported by a large labour force of mainly Russian and French prisoners.

The revier for prisoners of war was five minutes' walk from the station and had been adapted, as a kind of Cottage Hospital, from a large villa standing in its own grounds, once the property of a Jewish Doctor. Now, with its fences reinforced by barbed wire, it stood out as something different from the villas adjacent in the road, and especially from a bakery on one side of it from which issued tantalising, mouth-watering smells.

Architecturally it was fanciful, with a pepper-pot tower perched on one end and exaggerated gables. But it was solidly built, with thick walls, big cellars and strong shutters for the windows.

Most of the rooms on the ground floor were furnished with double-decker wooden bunks for the patients, the apparently inevitable accommodation for sick prisoners, probably determined by consideration, here, of available space. One room served as an orderly room for the Germans and for sick parades. At the rear they had their accommodation, and there were good facilities for gas cooking and decent sanitary arrangements. Upstairs, on the first floor was a bathroom with geyser and shower, a surgery, quite well equipped, the doctor's bed-sitting room heated by a wood-burning stove, and accommodation for the medical orderlies. On the top floor were more wards.

It was infinitely better than anything I had yet been in in Germany. A house and garden with electricity, hot-water and gas had it over a barrack hut anywhere, any time. True the ward windows were netted with barbed wire, but the Doctor's bed-sitter had French windows opening onto a balcony, to which we had free access during daylight hours. The room itself was rectangular with two real spring beds on either side, a long table down the middle between the beds, two desks with table lamps at the balcony end, and a large cupboard and green-tiled stove at the other.

Living in the revier were five Germans; one corporal in charge, three privates and a sanitäte. The latter was aged about fifty and proved not to be very bright. The prisoner staff, apart from the newly arrived French doctor and myself, consisted of two British medical orderlies, two French orderlies and a Curé, and one Polish orderly who spoke very good French and Russian.

The previous doctors had left before we arrived so there was no proper hand-over of patients, or of hints and tips. But my French colleague, having already done a stint here in the past, soon made himself at home, while I hastened to button-hole the two British orderlies to learn what I could. They had both been taken in the western desert; Alex, a friendly, round-faced, sturdy Scot, Larry, a laconic, lean, sandy-haired South African with a strong Boer accent. I introduced myself apologetically.

'I've only been in the bag a little short of two months and am pretty green when it comes to the ins and outs of POW life. I'll have to lean on you chaps a lot until I get the feel of things here.'

'Don't you worry, Sir,' said Alex, 'We've got it wrapped. Wouldn't you say Larry?

'Tight as a drum, mate. Tight as a drum.'

'Tell me about my work load.'

Alex grinned, 'hardly amounts to a load. Twenty-two beds here, not always full, three sick-parades a week downstairs and, on alternate days, three sick parades at Grimma.'

'Grimma?'

'A town ten miles down the line towards Dresden. We take the train. Not a bad day's outing.'

'And the parcel situation?'

'Not as good as it has been. We've put ourselves on half rations and have enough to last us about two months, assuming the worst and no more get through. But there are plenty of fresh vegetables, we keep rabbits, trade with the Jerries and get bread from the bakery next door. We're on good terms with the locals. Most of them seem to hope we shall win the war, and the sooner the better. They're all for the quiet life.'

'What's the form for the rest of today?'

'The other MOs held the sick parade before they left. It'll just be a ward round here this afternoon.'

'Now?'

'If you like, sir.'

I was anxious to get to grips with the work and to get to know the patients. Alex and Larry accompanied me upstairs to where the British sick were and we slowly went round, visiting each bunk in turn. I examined all the case-sheets, carefully written up by the outgoing doctor with comments on future management. There was nothing very serious. The worst were a few cases of bronchitis and gastroenteritis, already on the mend. The majority were relatively minor ailments, 'flu', sinusitis, acute piles, varicose ulcers. I breathed a sigh of relief. Nothing I could not handle – yet.

It was a fine day and Alex suggested we took a walk.

'Just like that?'

'Why not? Show you round a bit.'

'No guards?'

'Lord no. Just have to clear it with the Obergefreite and tell him when we'll be back. Shall we say an hour and a half? Larry'll keep an eye on the patients. He's got his rabbits to feed and hutches to clear out.'

'OK, fine.'

We turned left out of the gate, unlocked for us by the sanitäte. There was a bell on one of the posts we were to ring on our return.

'Facing north now,' said Alex. The station's to the north-east, the Rathaus to the north-west.'

We ambled through the streets, Alex frequently stopping to chat with some of the natives, took a look at the Rathaus set on the west side of the cobbled Platz, and then walked a short way down the road to Leipzig, off which we turned right and followed a country footpath. There were still a few leaves clinging to the deciduous trees, intermingled with pines and firs, and it was very pleasant to be breathing the sharp, fresh air and enjoying country sights and sounds.

'It strikes me,' I said, 'they're almost inviting us to try to escape.'

'But they know we won't,' Alex was quick to reply. 'There's an unwritten rule among medics at this stalag that we don't foul it up for others by trying it on. The Germans crack down at once if any of us went on walking. Post all the other medics to lock-up camps and leave the British sick to the tender mercies of the Jerry docs or those of other nationals.

'A chap got out of Colditz,' I said. 'Made it to the Swiss border. Did you know?'

Alex looked at me anxiously. I think he thought because of my red beret and parachute wings I must be a reckless type. I hastened to reassure him.

'If that's the form here I'll stick with it, for the time being. But you realise circumstances are bound to change. Once the Allies are over the Rhine, the last major obstacle, they'll move fast in this direction. We'll find ourselves in a squeeze situation between them and the Russkis. Hard to know what the rules will be then.' I changed the subject. 'Your German seems very good. I've got to improve mine fast. Got any ideas?'

Alex looked pleased. 'You've come to the right place. We've got the full set of linguaphone records and study books for German at the revier, together with phrase books, grammars and dictionaries. The Obergefreite'll let you read his daily paper. It's a load of rubbish but simple to understand. It'll pay you to look up all the words you don't know and note the slang. It'll come quicker than you think.' He looked at his watch. 'Time to go back. I'll give you a sort of lesson on the way if you like. Glebens Leben will want you to talk to him about the cases in German.'

'Glebens Leben? Who's that?'

'Oberstabsarzt Glebens Leben. Commands a Jerry military hospital the other end of the town from here and, unfortunately, Oberstabsarzt Glebens bloody Leben is the Jerry MO who commands our outfit.'

'Like that is it?'

'He's the big fly in the ointment. Can be very awkward. You have to have all the case notes duplicated in German for him when he visits, usually once, sometimes twice a week. I generally write them out and the sanitäte types them for him. Now, imagine you're in the ward. He comes up and points to a patient, 'Was is das' 'what's this?' he says. You say 'er hat', 'he has,' and then tell him your diagnosis. If it's an 'itis' it will be an "entzündung", "Blasenentzündung", bladder infection, "Ohrentzündung", ear infection, easy really ...'

Alex went on with his simplifications of the language as we strolled back to the revier, setting me straight on pronunciation, and making me repeat short sentences to do with medical matters. We rang the bell and were duly let in. Upstairs in the doctor's room the stove was giving out a cheerful heat, and a satisfactory meal by prisoner standards soon appeared which we tucked into with relish. I thought of Pip Smith and the others still at Falingbostel, but my comparative comfort and afflu-ence brought on a feeling of guilt. So I stopped thinking of him. I had struck very lucky, or so it seemed. But there is always a joker in the pack. That night the French doctor and I were eaten alive by bed-bugs.

Next morning we complained bitterly to the Obergefreite, or rather the French doctor did in his fluent German. The Obergefreite was quite unimpressed and totally disbelieving, and we were obliged to submit ourselves to the indignity of divesting ourselves of our garments and displaying the bites.

'Floh,' he said derisively, then gabbled some more I did not under-stand.

'Que'st que c'est Floh – que'st qu'il dit?' I asked my colleague

'Il dit que nous avons apporté puces ici ... brought fleas with us here. He says we must have done because the other doctors never complained of being bitten.'

'If we had fleas on us we would have felt them before. I'm sure they were bed bugs. Do you not agree?'

'Bien sur.'

'Then we should insist on having new mattresses and the room fumi-gated.'

'D'accord ... perhaps the others were immune or the bugs fancied a change of diet.'

It was hard going trying to persuade the Obergefreite to do what we wanted but in the end, reluctantly, he produced some sulphur and fumi-gated our room with such German thoroughness that the fumes lingered in our nostrils for days afterwards.

I did a round of the patients, and then had the rest of the time before the midday meal to myself. The old wind-up gramophone needed fre-quent needle changes, but was just about able to cope with the lingua-phone records and I applied myself, as in every possible free moment, to working my way through them. The Obergefreite was pleased to lend me his paper, the *Algemeine Zeitung*, but it meant very little to me yet. I got Alex to take me through that part of it referring to the war situation, identifying key words which I wrote down, and later looked up in the dictionary to fix them in my mind. German had been a subject I could have taken at school and now very much wished I had, but for some reason best known to himself my form-master directed me into Spanish, a language I had enjoyed learning but was utterly useless to me now. But I had a very good memory, one that had served me well in my medical examinations and stood me in good stead in a reasonably rapid acquisition of passable German.

The afternoon found Alex, one of the German private soldiers and myself on our way to Grimma. We walked the short distance to the station and boarded a train. Alex chatted quite freely with some of the other passengers, and especially with the ticket collector, a Fraulein with whom he appeared to be on very friendly terms.

'She wants to know,' he said to me, 'what that red beret and French overcoat signify. I've told her you're a paratrooper doctor, Fallschirmjäger Arzt.'

I thought I would try out some German. 'Ich bin Englander, nicht Frei Franzose. Ha, Ha.'

'Ha Ha?' She smiled, 'nicht frei irgundetwas. Du bist gefangene, pechvogel.'

'What's that she's saying'?'

Alex chuckled. 'You're not a free anybody. You're a prisoner, unlucky fellow.'

'Too right.' but I smiled back at her as she made to continue her way down the train, and tried again, politely, 'Ich hoffe, Sie bald wieder su sehen.'

'Bis Donnerstag. Auf wiedersehen.'

'She's always on this train the days we go to Grimma. Likes a chat,' said Alex.

At Grimma, a more industrialised small town than Naunhof, we walked to a factory, in the precincts of which was a wooden hut set aside as a surgery for the prisoners who worked there. I stood at one end of the room, by a table, on which were the case notes, and beside which stood a German sanitäte. The sick-parade advanced towards me in a long shuffling queue. They were predominantly British, but with a few other nationals. Alex had already warned me the main thing they would want from me was a decision in favour of their being unfit for work, and that tales of woe would be produced to ensure, if possible, that I would mark them down as 'nicht arbeitsfeht'.

'Terrible backache, sir.'

'Let's have a look.'

'Can't bend very well.'

'Try.'

'Hurts too much.'
'here?' I prodded. 'Not exactly.'
'here?'
'No.'
'here?'
'Oh yes. That's it. Terrible pain.'

Alex, meanwhile, was translating to the German sanitäte the details of the proceedings. He had also told me that the Germans knew all too well the majority of men reporting sick were only trying to get off work, and would not accept an unfit for work sick rate above a certain level, somewhere about ten-per-cent. As much as I might sympathise it was impossible to give all of them what they wanted. Too many off work and the sanitäte would report to Glebens Leben, who would attend my next sick-parade in person and take the decisions out of my hands, to the very possible detriment of those who were genuinely sick.

It was a quite new game for me. In England, the parachute battalion to which I was medical officer was so keen to distinguish itself in action that malingering was almost unknown, and quite conspicuous by its absence if there was the slightest rumour of impending operations. I realised I was going to have to sharpen my clinical perception considerably. I had to make sure, at least, that I spotted the genuinely unfit and secured relief for them.

The sanitäte gave a fierce warning look at every man as he came before me, searching faces, and every now and again barking at Alex, who passed his remarks on to me.

'He says this man is sick too often. He's already had enough time off work. He wants to know exactly what is wrong with him.'

At this particular juncture the man in question had his arm in a sling. He took it out gingerly and displayed it, wrapped in a voluminous paper bandage. I unwound it carefully, the man wincing at each turn. Underneath, the whole of the lower forearm was covered in a thick layer of what looked like black treacle, and which my nose told me was a preparation of ichthammol.

'What's the trouble?'
'Me arm's festering, sir.'
'How did it start?'
'Bad injury at work, sir.'
'Where exactly is it?'
'Under 'ere.' He pointed to a spot above his wrist.

I tore off a piece of the paper bandage and gently wiped off the black stuff until I could properly see the skin, the man all the while grimacing and sucking air in through his closed teeth. Eventually all that was revealed was a very tiny sore.

'Who advised the treatment for this?' I asked.

'The other MO who came last week.'

'Well, his treatment has been very successful. Have you been off work since then?'

'Yessir,' said the man reluctantly.

'All you need now is a bit of strapping, and be careful not to knock it again.'

He gave me a baleful look. 'Back to work, is it then?'

'Afraid so.'

He slouched off morosely.

'He'll be back again soon.' Alex spoke quietly into my ear. 'It's self-inflicted. The next time he comes it'll be all red and raw and you'll be able to take him off work without objections from Jerry. They'll be watching him closely in the factory to try to catch him in the act, as they do the others, but the lads are too smart for them, you'll find even more of this sort of thing at Naunhof where they work mostly in a stone quarry. Easy to drop large bits on your feet or hands. Sometimes they go as far as to break fingers or toes. A painful but sure way of evading work, Jerry may well suspect half the accidents are phoney, but once you've put them in a plaster splint they can't argue the toss about them being unfit.'

I took a long time over this first sick parade, fearful I might overlook a *bona fide* illness. Of the thirty or so men who attended there were five who should have been in bed, and at the end of it Alex said we had to visit the Lager where there were some in their bunks too ill to attend the parade. These turned out to be the kind of cases I already had in Naunhof revier. I was again taking my time when Alex nudged me to get a move on, sir, our train leaves in twenty minutes. I gave him a helpless look.

'Don't worry, sir, we'll be back here the day after tomorrow.'

I did a skimpy superficial examination of the remainder, Alex writing up my treatments for the German sanitäte, and we made off at a smart pace for the station. Once seated Alex commented,

'It was a bigger parade then usual. I suspect they knew there was a new MO coming and thought they'd try you on. Normally we get through in plenty of time to have a cup of coffee and chat up the sanitäte. You'll soon get the hang of it.'

I hope so, I thought fervently, as the train returned us to Naunhof through the darkening countryside. The word has got round, a new MO. They'll all want to know what he's like, what sort of doctor. Trouble is I don't really know myself. I recalled the padre's words at Oschatz, 'discretion and impartiality, they must feel they can always confide in you'. I've somehow got to make the malingerers know I'm always on their side against the Germans, at the same time keeping the Germans at bay. What really matters, I went on thinking, is that a genuinely sick man gets the treatment he needs, and for that I'll have to win the respect of the Germans for my clinical judgement. It's going to be tricky tight-rope job. Hope I don't fall off.

At the sick parade at Naunhof next morning the proceedings were brought to an unheralded halt by the arrival of Oberstabsarzt Glebens Leben. The Obergefreite called us all to attention as he walked slowly down the room in my direction, treating each of the prisoners to a hard stare of inspection as he passed along the queue. Alex stepped forward and handed me over as if on a parade ground.

'Guten Morgen Herr Oberstabsarzt. Das ist Captain Mawson Royal Army Medical Corps.'

Glebens Leben extended a grey-gloved hand, which I took and held momentarily as he withdrew it on contact, without shaking, and waved it airily in the direction of the patients.

'Bitte. Fortfahren.'

He was aged about fifty-five, thick-set, with a large nose, narrow-spaced eyes and sallow complexion, unprepossessing to say the least. He stationed himself at my left elbow, his hands folded below his belt, and watched as I nervously fumbled my way through the interviews. There was again a large number reporting sick, at which he expressed displeasure, and every now and then he would check me with a question relayed through Alex, and once or twice he reversed decisions I had made regarding fitness for work. Alex stood staunchly by acting as a kind of buffer between us, translating as a running commentary the demands of Glebens Leben as I examined each patient. I felt as I had when undergoing the clinical part of my finals in London, clumsy and thick-headed, sure I was failing to impress either the men or the Oberstabsarzt. Two hours later, when I had at last got to the end of the queue, he delivered his verdict.

'I commend you on your thoroughness but you are inclined to be far too lenient. You must adopt exactly the same standards as we have in the German Army.' I had heard this before, 'many of the men you marked as unfit for work,' he continued with a disdainful expression, 'would be in our front line fighting for the Fatherland.'

I began to feel a combative urge rising within me but suppressed it, instinct telling me this first encounter with him was not the moment to sound off. I turned to Alex.

'Would you thank the Oberstabsarzt for his guidance, and tell him I will endeavour to remember his instructions.'

Glebens Leben eyed me narrowly, and said a few more words, the gist of which, I was able to gather, was that he now wanted me to show him the patients upstairs in bed. I got through this without any comment from him whatever, which was, paradoxically, more unnerving than his interruptions at the parade. But at the door, to which Alex escorted him, while I stood to attention beside the nearest bunks, he turned and barked at me, watching the effect of his words while Alex translated.

'Remember what I have ordered you. German army standards. Malingerers are not tolerated. I will not tolerate them. You will not tolerate them.'

I said nothing and kept my face neutral, hoping he would take it as a sign of acquiescence. But he wanted more than that.

'Verstehen Sie?'

'Ich habe verstanden.'

'Gut.' Upon which he turned on his heel and abruptly departed.

I had understood well enough but I had not compromised my position. All I had actually said in the course of the morning was I would endeavour to remember his instructions. I felt I was still on the rope.

'How do you think that went?' I asked Alex.

'OK, but he means every word. He'll do his best next time to catch you out. I've seen all this before. He gives his warning and if he doesn't think you are toeing the line he goes all parade-ground. Whatever happens don't let him rile you. I've heard shouting matches go on here between him and other British MOs. You can't beat him that way. You'll just get posted.'

'But I've got to protest if he overrules me on a point of fitness when I think I am right, and I must have the prisoners believe I am on their side. How do I protest without him getting shirty?'

'The way the French doctors do. Preface everything with the politest possible remarks, like, "With the utmost respect Herr Oberstabsarzt, I find myself in distasteful but unavoidable disagreement". He laps up any amount of that sort of thing. I'll teach you some of the choice phrases this afternoon.'

'Agree when I can. Disagree when I must, but never be disagreeable.'

'That's just about it.'

I thought of Bill Alford and Pip Smith bearding Möglich in his den and demanding their rights, and here I was being coached in a kind of abject diplomacy. But thinking on a bit further there were some valid differences in our circumstances. They had had the advantage, in one case, of superiority, in the other of equality of rank, whereas I was junior to Glebens Leben, and in point of fact the medical facilities provided here were well up to Geneva Convention standards. I was not engaged in a fight for rights, but in a fencing match over malingerers. I would be thrusting, Glebens Leben parrying. If he chose to riposte he could always win the point, so it would be unwise to needle him too hard. I might come to relish the contest as adding a dimension to life that would at least ensure it was never dull.

Thus the pattern of life at Naunhof unfolded itself. I made rapid strides with the language, being increasingly able to manage my engagements with Glebens Leben in his own tongue. He never failed to remind me that I was where I was on sufferance, his sufferance and that I was to regard myself as fortunate to be allowed to practice my profession under his jurisdiction. I trod very carefully to avoid his corns, never pushing my luck too far when he was around, but nevertheless chalking up a steady tally of off-work victories. The sanitäte was fairly easy meat. Alex knew how to humour him and would engage him in a steady flow of banter, while I would quietly ask each man in the queue, 'are you ill or do you just want "off"?' If he were to reply, 'off', I might say loudly, 'sprained wrist here Alex, strapping and sling. Unfit. One week.' The men would play the part. Larry would strap him up, and I would go on to the next one. A time might come when Alex would signal with his fingers, ten-per-cent. Then I would have to tell the 'offs' to come another time, in case there were some 'genuines' still in the queue.

On Glebens Leben days I was punctilious, and sometimes would approach him deferentially and ask his clinical opinion of a case I was examining. He was a hospital doctor and tended to regard anything not requring admission to hospital as verging on the perfectly fit. But I discovered I could arouse in him a genuine interest in the detection and interpretation of physical signs. I would ask him to listen to a chest in which I was sure I could hear abnormal sounds, and it pleased him to put his finger on the spot, and to tell me there was no doubt about it, and to put my stethoscope just there. We operated in an atmosphere of undoubted mutual antagonism, the inevitable enmity engendered by the war, and we had our arguments, but the temperature never rose to boiling point. I could but attempt the practical co-existence that was required of me with its built-in restraints. I was uneasy with it, a false and fragile peace, but at Naunhof it held.

The thrice-weekly train journey to Grimma added variety to the day-to-day routine, and gave me an opportunity to observe the German people – civilians – at first hand. As I grew ever more proficient in their language I was able to listen in to their conversations, which referred constantly to the difficulties in their lives, rationing, heating, regimentation, air-raids, but were never defeatist. They might express weariness with the war, and dissatisfaction with some of the ways things were being run, but I never heard any open criticism of Hitler, or anything to indicate a lack of faith in the leadership, or the performance of their army. The Luftwaffe was another matter. Of the Allied air forces there was evidence in plenty, the Americans by day, the British by night. In Naunhof little heed was paid to the sirens which nearly always went off at some time during the twenty-four hours. In the revier we wondered vaguely if the whereabouts of the two factories making Messerschmitt parts was known to the Allies, but they were some two miles away and we never felt Naunhof would rank as a primary target. The Luftwaffe was conspicuous only by its absence. I never once saw any attempt to interfere with our machines. It became a standing joke among the civilians that if a German aeroplane should happen to fly over it was a sure sign there were none of the Allies in the offing. A German fighter had been shot down by an American in September and crashed a few hundred yards from the station; this, in the heartland of Germany, had made a considerable impression on the inhabitants. One day, after a large formation of Flying Fortresses had passed over, I asked the Obergefreite,

'Warum kein Luftwaffe?'

He shrugged his shoulders.

'Luftwaffe kaput.'

I thought he might be about to add 'alles kaput' but, while liberal in his treatment of ourselves, he maintained, at this time, an unbroken front of confidence in the ultimate outcome of the war in Germany's favour. A shrug of the shoulders was symbolic of the general attitude. 'I do not like what is happening but what can I do about it?' The Fraulein ticket collector summed it all up for me.

'Why should I worry? I can still work. I can still eat, and I can still make love.'

An interesting sequence of priorities.

I had been at Naunhof just ten days when my French doctor colleague with the toothbrush moustache was unaccountably transferred elsewhere and replaced by another, much younger man almost his exact opposite in attitude and character. Whereas the first was rotund, humorous, realistic, relaxed and cynical, the second was thin, idealistic, intense and serious. He wore glasses, giving him a studious appearence, and had had his hair cut Prussian-style, rising up very short and straight from his head, purposely, he told me, to make his appearance more notable. He had been a prisoner since the collapse and occupation of France and spoke the language of his captors perfectly, but he disliked them intensely and had been up before three disciplinary tribunals for being too outspoken. At the same time he had also been commended by the Chefarzt for bravery in extinguishing incendiary bombs dropped by the RAF in a raid on

Leipzig, that had landed on the roof of the infirmary, the one I visited, when he had been working there. He was volatile and unpredictable in his reactions and moods but a fine doctor, putting the interests of the prisoners before any other consideration, and whose medical knowledge and skill was considerable. He knew the Germans and their weaknesses inside out and how to exploit them, and was totally familiar with all the tortuous red-tape and turgid bureaucratic paperwork that went with the job of being a POW doctor.

I took to Jean at once and soon found him, foremost, a very good friend and companion, but not least from my point of view, a mine of useful information and sound advice. The French prisoners loved him (he had served at Naunhof before) and used to bring him presents of food whenever they had the chance, which was not infrequent for, unlike the British in the stone quarries, the French were doing agricultural work on farms, or else assisting the butchers, bakers and dairymen in their shops. For them the purloining of edibles was as much a sport, when it was not a grim necessity, as listening to the BBC was for us. These personal gifts of food he used to have made up by a French cook into the most astoundingly ingenious and delicious dishes, and since we shared board and lodging I benifited hugely from his popularity. In return I put my Red Cross parcels into our common store, for the French were not receiving any. Alex, and Larry too, when it came to supplementing the rations, were not without their resources. Nearly every household in Naunhof kept rabbits for food, and Larry was the jealous possessor of the most virile buck in the whole neighbourhood. The buck's services were eagerly sought after, and Larry's servicing charge was always another rabbit. Alex negotiated the steady flow of clandestine assignations and, since the Obergefreite and other Germans in the revier were beneficiaries in the forn of rabbit portions for their own pot, the trade, although technically quite illegal, flourished.

One day Jean and I were approached by the Obergefreite on behalf of a German officer who had recently acquired a puppy, and whose tail he wished to have docked. Would we oblige?

'Why not?' said Jean.

'The officer will be very grateful,' said the Obergefreite, 'and will pay you a fee in marks. But of course their must be no mention of it.' We agreed a date, the coming Sunday, and a time, eleven o'clock in the morning after the patients had been seen to. Jean spoke very little English and we always conversed in French. I had told him, after the war, I hoped to take up surgery as a career, and he suggested I should operate on the tail while he administered an anaesthetic He decided to use ethyl chloride as it was readily available, as a freezing agent to spray on the skin for

85

minor procedures such as stitching cuts or lancing boils. It seemed quite appropriate as I had seen it used when dropped onto a gauze mask to induce sleep in children. The puppy, a small mongrel terrier of uncertain ancestry, was duly delivered in a straw-strewn cardboard box, and we carried him up to the treatment room adjacent to our bed-sitter. We were now into early December, it was very cold, and the stove in the treatment room was kept going night and day, one of Larry's chores.

We put the little dog onto the operating table, Jean put a few drops of ethyl chloride onto a gauze pad and applied it to his muzzle. It wriggled all over the place at first but soon became still.

'OK' said Jean, 'il dors. Vous pouvez commencer.'

I thought I would try to make a first-class job of the amputation, leaving a surplus flap of skin to sew over the stump. I made a careful, bevelled incision with the scalpel and started to disarticulate the selected joint. It was all very easy. Too easy. Something began to nag at me. Something was wrong. Then the penny dropped. There was no bleeding. I turned to Jean.

'J'ai peur. Il n'y a pas du sang. Est ce qu'il est OK?'

Jean removed the gauze from the animal's muzzle, whipped a stethoscope out of his pocket and applied it frenziedly to the heart area, listening first here then there. Then he slowly took the instrument out of his ears, looked at me with a sombre expression on his face and said gravely,

'Mon Dieu. Le petit chien est mort.'

'Oh my Lord. What now? What is the German officer going to say?'

Jean remained calm. 'He is not going to say anything because he is not going to know anything about it – yet. Finish the amputation my friend. We must let it be thought that the operation has been a complete successs. We will show the tail to the Obergefreite, and give instructions that on no account must anyone enter the room and disturb the dog as he is still recovering from the anaesthetic. We will put him back in his box, near the stove, and keep him there until tomorrow. Sew up the stump as you planned. That's it. Now curl him up in the box, natural sleeping position. Good.'

'Larry will have to be told about it,'I said, 'he has to come in here to stoke up the stove last thing at night.'

Jean thought for a moment. 'Agreed. But you must swear him to secrecy. He can let it be known the dog was alive and well when he paid his last visit to the stove.'

'What about tomorrow?'

'Larry can put out the same report first thing in the morning. Sometime later I will discover the dog has had a sudden unexpected heart failure and you will call the Obergefreite. When you both arrive you will find me doing everything possible to rescuscitate him. You will be visibly upset. The Germans know the English reputation for being animal lovers, and I will remind him of it as you wring your hands and shed your tears.

'Wait a bit,' I said, 'isn't that overdoing it. I'm not all that good an actor.'

'You will surpass yourself. The Obergefreite will be so affected he will advise the German officer to pay our fee in spite of the tragedy. You will see.'

'The dog must have had a weak heart in the first place to succumb to such a small dose of anaesthetic.'

'Precisely. That is the conclusion. He was a weakling. Never a fit companion for a German officer.'

Jean and I took the tail down to the Obergefreite.

'The operation is over and the puppy is sleeping off the anaesthetic,' said Jean, without batting an eyelid. 'We wondered if the officer would like the tail. It belongs to him.'

'Oh no,' said the Obergefreite, 'that can go in this stove.'

He suited the action to his words. 'But he will want the dog back as soon as possible.'

'It is best he stays here the night, and is left entirely undisturbed. He will not need feeding. It would only make him sick. What he needs is a good long sleep now. Tomorrow he will still feel rather shaky. Perhaps the officer will be pleased to collect him in the afternoon?'

'Sehr gud, und vielen Dank.'

The treatment room was normally kept locked when not in use. There were three keys, one held by the Obergefreite, one by ourselves, and the other by the medical orderly on stove duty. I hastened to find Larry to put him in the picture.

'Oh my old Transvaal,' he was nearly doubled up laughing, 'don't you worry meinheer. I'll tell the bloody kaffers the dog's as fit as a springbok. This'll kill the boys when they hear of it.'

'Nobody's to hear of it,' I said sharply, 'not even Alex. Only you're to know.'

He looked at me askance. 'Seems a shame. Waste of a bloody fine joke – but if you say so.'

'OK then?'

'OK.'

Everything went according to plan. Larry duly, casually let slip to the Obergefreite that the dog was in good shape last thing that night and first thing on the Monday morning, when he made his report as duty orderly.

We held the usual sick parade. There were one or two patients needing attention in the treatment room whom we held back until the end. Then we went upstairs, the patients, Alex and Larry, and a French orderly following. Jean unlocked the door.

'How's the pup?' I asked according to our prearranged scenario.

Jean advanced on the box, looked in, looked away, hurriedly looked in again, then dropped precipitously on one knee beside it. He felt the animal, lifted it up, felt it again, put it back in the box and turned to me, his face a picture of startled incredulity.

'Je pense, pertetre qu'il est presque mort!'

'Oh no!'

'Can't be,' said Larry 'he was quite OK this morning.'

'Get the Obergefreite.'

I ran down the stairs, shouting his name. He met me at the bottom.

'What is it?'

'Come at once. We are concerned about the puppy.'

In the treatment room we found Jean rhythmically compressing the dog's chest. On seeing us he shook his head sadly.

'It is no good. His heart 'as stopped.' He hesitated, searching for the right German words, 'why, I cannot understand.'

I knelt by Jean's side and took the stethoscope, probing here and there. 'No doubt about it,' I said in a mournful tone, taking the corpse and cradling it in my arms. 'Poor little hound, poor little hound. What a shame.' I managed to get a break into my voice. 'Here, Jean. You take him. I can't bear to see him like this.' I retreated from the scene and went and stood by the window. Jean returned the dead puppy to its box, which he handed to the Obergefreite,

'Doctor Mawson is overcome. He was so enchanted with the puppy. You know how the English are with animals.'

The Obergefreite nodded, his own face now wearing a very sad expression.

'I am afraid,' continued Jean, 'there must have been an inherited weakness. It would have shown itself sooner or later. Please convey our deepest sympathy to the German officer. There is nothing more we could have done to save him. Would you like us to bury him in the garden?'

'We will do it.' The Obergefreite took the box and solemnly bore it out of the room.

'I say. What a shame.' said Alex.

I returned from the window. 'Can't be helped. Just one of those things. Best get on with the treatments.'

Larry gave me a surreptitious wink which I returned with a stern look of warning.

'OK Larry?'

'OK.'

We heard no more from the Obergefreite about the incident. As we got ready for bed I twitted Jean,

'What about our fee, the Marks then?'

Jean looked serious.

'I would not have accepted in any case. We had bad luck with the little dog, and bad luck always goes in threes. We had better look out.'

The very next day, in the late morning, we were sitting in our room reading when Jean's orderly knocked on the doors and came in with an urgent call for him to see a French prisoner brought in with a badly cut hand. Jean leapt to his feet and made for the door and somehow managed to collide with the orderly, staggered, hit the side of his head against the door itself, knocking his spectacles onto the floor, whereupon the orderly, in trying to regain his own balance, promptly trod on them. The result was awesome. Jean flew into a perfectly furious storm of rage.

'My spectacles, my spectacles!' he cried, swaying from side to side, with his hands cupped to the side of his eyes like a set of horses blinkers. 'My only pair. I am a blind man!' He gave the orderly a rough push in the chest. 'You clumsy fellow! Stupid oaf! Pick up the pieces! It is a disaster.' His eyes filled with tears of anger. He hammered his fist against the door, kicked it, and then threw himself face down on his bed and buried it in the pillow. I kept very quiet. Presently he sat up as if nothing untoward had happened.

'You know,' he said in his normal voice, 'it is the little dog, the bad luck.'

'The Germans will soon fix you up with another pair,' I offered hopefully.

'Bien sur, this very day.' he was quite calm now, and quite serious. 'Nevertheless, it was the little dog.'

Sod's law more like, I thought. Drop your piece of bread and jam on the carpet and it's bound to fall jam side down. But I knew I would never be able to explain that particular Anglicism to him, and he would only think me facetious. So instead I offered to go and treat his patient and tell the Obergefreite of his urgent need to visit the optician, and I suggested he rested quietly after his traumatic experience. He lay back, his hand clasped beneath his head and closed his eyes.

'Thank you. You are a good friend.'

The following Tuesday evening, on my return from Grimma, the Obergefreite motioned me into his office. An order had come through from the Chefarzt directing me to exchange duties with Captain Webster at the revier in Leipzig. I had enjoyed the afternoon out and was in a buoyant mood only, now, to feel myself suddenly, utterly downcast.

'You are sure there is no mistake?'

'No mistake. Here is the order. Read it for yourself.'

I felt myself fated to be uprooted the moment I had really settled down. I was content at Naunhof, and had built up a good relationship with the prisoners in the few weeks I had been here. Now I was to be installed in the one place I had been so glad not to be going to when I last visited it. I conceded that Webster needed a rest. He had been there for over a year. But why me? Had I blotted my copy book with Glebens Leben in some way? I gloomily broke the news to Jean, who by now had acquired another pair of glasses. He looked at me with an I-told-you-so expression through the steel rims,

'It is the little dog, you know. First me. Now you.' He visibly brightened 'That's the third piece of bad luck. No more to come now.'

There was nothing I could do but make the best of it. Jean had served in the Leipzig revier on several occasions, and I pumped him for information.

'You will work very long hours. There are a lot of sick. There is a Boche doctor, a veritable pig, called Brettschneider who is the supervisor. You will have to fight him all the time.'

'What rank is he?'

'Stabsarzt.'

'Captain. Same as me.'

'Yes, but don't think he will treat you as an equal. He will expect you to toe his line. No leniency towards the prisoners. Far worse than Glebens Leben. But I have not been there for some months. Things may heve changed with the change in the German fortune of war.

'You know Captain Webster?'

'Oh, sure. We have been there together. I'll soon make him at home here.'

'Lucky devil,' I thought. I was definitely feeling sorry for myself and, recognising the fact, realised I had better snap out of it. Naunhof was a cushy billet, no doubt of that. If things were to be tougher I should at least be thankful I had had the time and chance to learn the ropes, and the language, and to ease myself gently into the saddle of single-handed medical practice among working prisoners-of-war in Germany.

VI

Leipzig
(14 December 1944 – 6 March 1945)

At dusk, in the evening of Thursday 14 December, having held my last sick parade at Grimma, said farewell to Jean, Alex, Larry and my patients at Naunhof, and been escorted by a guard back to Leipzig, I stood once again outside the forbidding façade of the revier, Gneisenau Strasse, York Platz.

The guard rang the bell, the door was opened by a German private, and I stepped over the threshold into the stone-walled entrance hall. The private opened a door on my left, and I was ushered into the Feldwebel's orderly room, or administrative office. Webster was there, sitting reading a newspaper. He sprang up, pumped my hand and looked at my face for a long moment.

'You look indecently fit and well-fed. Naunhof seems to have agreed with you.'

'Yes, I've quite enjoyed it there.' Webster himself looked strained and frail. 'How have things been with you?'

'Oh, as bloody as usual. I don't mind telling you, I'm ready for a change. When they told me I was going to Naunhof it was the best news I heard for months.' He turned to the sergeant who had risen from his desk at my entry. 'Feldwebel, this is Captain Mawson. You remember he visited us a few weeks ago on his way to Naunhof.'

I acknowledged the introduction with a slight, stiff bow, which the Feldwebel returned with a serious, but not unfriendly expression on his face.

'Must go at once, now you're here. Your guard's taking me. We've to catch the last train.' He shook my hand again. 'Best of luck old man. See you sometime perhaps.' The Feldwebel gestured my late guard to help carry some of Webster's gear, clapped the latter on the shoulder and bundled them both out of his office and into the street without more ado.

Webster, at my previous visit, had filled me in on the Feldwebel, who was a short, grey-haired, roughish-looking man in his late fifties 'A decent enough fellow,' Webster had said. 'POW himself in England in the last war, and had his only son killed in the army in this.'

More significantly he was purely a Wehrmacht man who went by the book, was very correct, and not unsympathetic towards the British. He was in charge of the revier under Brettschneider, to whom he was responsible for our security, and for whom, Webster had intimated, his dislike was only matched by that of the medical staff. He ran his eye over my papers, commenting here and there, and asking me the odd question about my movements since being captured. Then he motioned me to a chair, and ordered a clerk, hitherto busy on a typewriter, to 'go and fetch van Eck,'

'Who is van Eck?' I ventured.

'Your interpreter.'

'My interpreter? I can manage a bit of German.'

'You have to travel all over Leipzig to visit prisoners. He will see you do not get lost or into trouble.'

I gazed round the office. There was a large map of the city on one wall, spattered with coloured pins bearing numbered paper flags.

'May I look?'

The Feldwebel explained. 'Here,' he pointed to a flag, 'is the revier. There are two big POW hospitals; and these others are the lagers.'

I spent some time trying to get my bearings. I did not like our proximity to the station, a fairly short walk and only a few minutes' tram ride away, as it obviously constituted a prime target for Allied bombers. Next to this map was another, of the whole of Germany, divided into square zones by a series of grid-lines, each zone carrying a name and number. Then my attention was taken by a thick cardboard plan of the building depicting the wards, with slotted pockets representing bunks, and a ticket in the slots bearing the name, lager number and diagnosis of each occupant. There was accommodation for sixty patients; twenty-two British, twenty French and eighteen Russian.

'Twenty-two patients,' I said, commenting really to myself, 'doesn't seem a lot. Same as Naunhof.'

But the Feldwebel, whose English turned out to be rather better than my German, picked me up. 'You are also responsible,' he said, for two thousand British, six hundred Dutch and five hundred Americans, working prisoners quartered in the numerous lagers. You hold three big sick parades here three mornings a week, and three mornings a week at Hasag, here,' he took me back to the flagged map and pointed out a location on the outskirts of the city, where I could see there was a high concentration of lagers, 'and every afternoon you visit lagers where there are men too sick to come to parades. You will find the work hard.'

'I've already been told that. Now I can well believe it.'

'But you have no official duties on Sundays.' The creases on the Feldwebel's face took on the outline of a smile, 'you can go out and amuse yourself if you want to.'

I could not imagine to what kind of amusement he was referring, nor what this battered city could possibly provide, but this was not, I felt, the moment to pursue the matter in detail.

Van Eck materialised as a young Dutch, ex-law student, fluent in English, French and German, with black crinkly hair, slightly arched eyebrows, and a square, pleasant, generally smiling face, although he would become morose and depressed at times; not that that was anything unusual among prisoners of war, escpecially those long separated from family and home. He took me up to the top floor where I had previously been entertained. The day's work was done, and all those who shared these quarters were gathered to welcome me. I felt very touched. Van Eck threw open the door and announced me with a flourish, upon which they all rose to their feet and, led by Médecin Capitaine Henri Denis, crowded round to shake my hand.

'Enchanté.'

'Enchanté.'

Another French doctor, Capitaine Bretiot from one of the main POW hospitals, a friend of Denis, and who would prove to be a frequent visitor, had come for the occasion. There were two resident French medical orderlies, le Maire and Petit, and David Kidd, an RAMC orderly from Yorkshire. This was the 'family', eating together and pooling resources, with French the common language.

Denis, thirty-seven years old, from the Saône et Loire region of France, had volunteered for service among French POWs and been in Leipzig for some months. He had arrived with suitcases full of clothes and was never less than impeccably turned out. He had a long, humorous face, dark, centrally parted, receding hair, and a trick of inclining his head toward his left shoulder whenever he smiled, which was often. He had the most elegant manners and politest turns of phrase. He was a most civilised person, determined to recreate for himself the style in which he was accustomed to live, teaching and helping us all thereby to try to ignore the reality of the straitened circumstances of our situation, which I was all too soon to discover. Without wanting to stretch the point too far, he put me in mind of the reputedly studied indifference to their fate exhibited by those prisoners of the French Revolution who were obliged to live under the shadow of the guillotine.

Petit, with his thin face, and le Maire with his round one, on the other hand, reminded me of Laurel and Hardy – without moustache. Denis was constantly chaffing them, using them as foils for his wit in a kindly way, and they acted up, exhibiting facial expressions of mock exasperation, frustration and injured innocence with gallic gestures to match. David, Webster had told me, was stirling stuff, apparently tireless and entirely dependable, and of the utmost importance to the revier as he had managed to acquire a radio able to pick up the BBC war bulletins. I sensed that David, in turn, had thought highly of Webster, and that I was going to have to rate with this Yorkshireman if things were to go well.

We had a meal, considerably more spartan than at Naunhof, and, Bretiot having taken his leave, prepared for bed. I shared a room with Denis looking out onto Gneisenau Strasse. Opposite was a block of apartments, at this time of the evening completely blacked out, as was the whole city. We had beds rather than bunks, but it was cold, very cold. Night frost was now the rule. There was no stove, the revier being nominally centrally heated. But there were strict fuel conservation measures in force in the city as everything had to be brought in by rail or road; unlike Naunhof where there was an abundance of wood available in the immediate countryside, and whose inhabitants, including the prisoners, made up their own collecting parties. I commented on the temperature to Denis. He shrugged his shoulders.

'This is only the beginning of the winter. They will turn the heat on again tomorrow for the sick-parade.'

'Tell me about the sick-parade arrangements.'

'Start at seven o'clock in the morning. Work through until finished. Time of that depends on the numbers. The Feldwebel and his clerks sit behind a long table at one end of the room, opposite the door. We stand in front of it. The sick form two queues and your line and mine simply advance side by side down the middle of the room towards us.

'Presumably they are in groups, from the various lagers?'

'Precisely, and each group is escorted by its own guard and sanitäte. When we have made our examination and recommendation we tell the Feldwebel. If it is only a question of medicine, the Feldwebel issues the sanitäte with the prescriptions for his party who draws them from our dispensary. If it is a matter of dressings or changes of plaster or something like that you do it yourself, you or David or one of our fellows. We help each other.'

'At Naunhof my main problem was with those pretending to be sick to get off work. Do many pretend sickness here?'

'Certainly, the majority; and Stabsarzt Brettschneider knows it, and we know it, and he knows we know it.' Denis smiled, cocking his head, and proceeded to light an evil-smelling Polish cigarette. A thought struck me.

'You have said the time we finish depends on the numbers. Can you give me any idea how many I might have to see?'

'Seldom less than one hundred and fifty. Sometimes two hundred.'

I gasped. 'Impossible. In one morning? Why,' I felt anger mounting within me, 'if I have to see two hundred patients and spend only three minutes with each, which is ten hours' work.'

'Agreed. So we can only afford two minutes. Then if we are lucky we may be finished by one o'clock in the afternoon and have time for something to eat before going out to visit the lagers.'

'My God,' I spluttered, 'I cannot work as fast as that!'

Denis softened the rather matter-of-fact tone of voice in which he had been speaking. 'Do not despair, my friend. The speed comes. It has to.' He stubbed out his cigarette, 'Now we had better sleep.'

Nil desperandum. Nil bloody *desperandum.* My mind churned over the seeming impossibility. Two minutes per patient. Well, we shall see. We shall just have to bloody well see.

Shortly after midnight the air-raid sirens started to wail up and down, exactly as in London; in fact I thought momentarily I was a medical student back in the blitz, but Denis switched on the light.

'Get up my friend. We have to put some clothes on in case it is necessary to descend to the cellar.'

I groaned. 'How often does this happen for goodness sake?'

'Oh, about every third night. We only have to take the patients and ourselves down if they are thought to be coming directly over.'

'And how often is that?'

'Not often. We have not been down for several weeks now.'

'A tiring precaution,' I said.

'You never know.'

We hung about for about twenty minutes, when the all-clear sounded and we returned to bed.

'Good night, again, then.'

'Good night.'

We rose at five-thirty, performed our ablutions, thankfully with hot water, and gathered in the mess room for breakfast; slices of black bread and ersatz butter from the Germans, jam and powdered coffee from the Red Cross parcels. Rationing in Leipzig was very strict as, like fuel, everything had to be brought in. There were none of the perquisites, the vegetable garden, the rabbits, the purloining from shops, as at Naunhof. For anything over and above the German provisions we were completely dependent on parcels. Denis' wife had been sending him regular consignments, mainly of dried fruit and nuts, and le Maire and Petit had had their family offerings. Bulky parcels for prisoners, whether Red Cross or personal, were very low on the priority list in the competition for space available in the overburdened and ever-diminishing rolling stock of the German railway system, and now, with the German retreat from France there was no longer a direct link with that country. All the parcels had to come through Switzerland, and. the stock-pile at the revier was now very low. There had been recent rumours of a resupply *en route* for the city. We could only hope there was some substance in it.

After breakfast Denis and I retired to our respective wards to do a round of the patients. It was necessary to discharge as many a possible before the sick-parade to free beds for those who might be found to need them that day. It was a hand-to-mouth system, often entailing moving men out to bed down in their lagers before their clinical condition ideally warranted it. The round took the best part of an hour, and then we descended to the big room for the start of the parade at seven o'clock.

'Brettschneider is certain to put in an appearance this morning,' predicted Denis, as we took up our station at the table, 'he will want to cast his eye over you. You have not met him before?'

'No.'

'He will hope to catch you out putting men off work who do not merit it to give him an excuse to dress you down. It would be best for you to toe the line today.'

'I take it he works to the usual upper limit of ten per cent?'

'Very much so. And the real sickness rate is on the increase, and we can expect it to get worse with winter. So the opportunities for giving off-work relief to the not-so-sick will diminish accordingly.'

I was going to be back on the tight rope; having to try to reconcile the main aim and object of the Germans, personified here in Brettschneider, to keep the prisoners at work for them, with the main aim and object of the prisoners, to avoid it. Most of them were engaged in repairing and rebuilding what the Allied air forces had knocked down, outdoor reconstruction work, hard labour at the best of times, rigorous now the winter had set in. It seemed likely I would be working in Leipzig until the war was over, and that it would be to the prisoners' advantage, as at Naunhof, if I could establish some sort of reputation with the Germans for realistic practice from the word go. The more they trusted me the freer the hand they would give me, and the more heed they would pay to any request I might have to make for special treatment, X-rays, transport for the sick, diets and other benefits. Much as I could sympathise with the 'malingerers', it was impossible to get them all off work. Indiscriminate handing out of certificates would immediately bring Brettschneider down on me, countermanding my recommendations and weakening, thereby, my authority with the prisoners, not to mention very likely posting me to an Oflag. Moreover if the word got round that I was a soft touch the size of my sick-parades would soon increase to unmanageable proportions. Thus I reasoned to myself. I must establish my own brand of understanding with the men, and work it the way I had before. The genuinely sick must have absolute priority, and the others save my precious time by making no pretence; not declaring themselves out in some fictitious complaint but saying outright they had come for time off. My chance for getting this policy known and accepted would come with my afternoon visits to the lagers. Meanwhile I would have to struggle through as best I could, and this morning, above all, keep the peace with Brettschneider.

Brettschneider came into the room after we had been at it for about two hours. Aged fifty or so, plump, pink, and balding, he wore rimless glasses, and a straggly, sandy-coloured moustache ill-concealing a poorly repaired hair-lip. Despite a well-cut uniform and polished jackboots in which he strutted down the room, his appearance was unimpressive. The proceedings were halted while Denis introduced us to each other; Brettschneider proffered a limp hand, threw me an unsmiling cold-eyed nod, and moved to behind the table where the Feldwebel was handling the case-notes.

'Carry on please.'

We carried on. Being anxious not to cause any misunderstanding between myself and the large body of men passing before me, I took every complaint at its face value, and questioned and examined every case with as much care and detail as time allowed. Every now and then Brettschneider came and stood over me at my elbow and asked questions which I answered out of the corner of my mouth as I concentrated on the job in hand. Once I turned to look at him and he seemed angry about something. But he said nothing and I got on with it. I was going absolutely flat out, keeping the off-work rate down to a reasonable number, and under the impression I was doing quite well, especially as he left the room after about an hour and a half without comment. But no sooner had the door closed behind him the Feldwebel came round from behind the table and beckoned me, with van Eck, to follow him.

'The stabsarzt wishes to see you in my office.'

It was like being back at school. I tried to hide my uneasiness.

'To congratulate me on my work do you think?'

'I do not think so.'

In the office Brettschneider glowered at me from in front of the Feldwebel's table against which he was leaning with folded arms, his bald head glistening with perspiration in the light shed from the window behind him. I stood to attention before him and waited. Suddenly he started shouting and spluttering.

'Does the English doctor consider he is affording sufficient respect to a German officer of senior rank who is good enough to speak to him, without standing and looking him properly in the face when he replies? Eh? Eh?'

He had got this out so fast and without pausing for breath that I wanted to ask him to repeat it more slowly so that I could properly take it in.

'I am afraid I do not understand Herr Stabsarzt.'

'This morning you behaved in an insulting manner and I demand an explanation.' Van Eck came to my rescue.

'Excuse me Herr Stabsarzt. May I explain to Captain Mawson?'

'Immediately please.'

'What he is getting at,' van Eck said earnestly and rapidly to me in English, 'is that when he spoke to you about your cases, you didn't bother to turn round to face him to answer him, and sometimes you didn't even stand up. The Germans are very touchy about rank and correct deportment in dealing with an officer.'

'Good Lord. I had no intention of insulting him.' I felt myself warming up, 'and in any case he isn't senior to me in rank. He should try getting through a sick parade the size of ours. He wouldn't, if he were in my place, want to waste time bobbing up and down or making sharp left turns every time I uttered.'

The Feldwebel began to look anxious. 'The stabsarzt is waiting.'

'What do you want me to answer?' said van Eck, 'Not what you've just said I hope.'

I thought rapidly. Best not to stir it up.

'Humble apologies, no offence meant, concentrating so hard on work, anything you think will mollify him.'

Van Eck conveyed what sounded to me like a sickeningly sycophantic, crawling string of placatory phrases which, nevertheless, seemed to have the desired affect. The Feldwebel's face unlined itself. Brettschneider relaxed his stance, but he could not restrain a final sneer.

'I hope you are not representative of the British army. I always understood officers and gentlemen prided themselves on their manners.'

Van Eck said nothing, hoping, he told me later, I had not fully understood Brettschneider's remark. But I had, and it was my turn to go red in the face. It has been my misfortune on many occasions to react hastily, to utter words I have later much regretted. The situation was to me very provoking. Van Eck could see it, and again came to my rescue by laying a restraining hand on my right arm. His touch steadied me. I held on to myself, took a deep breath and said, quietly, in my best German.

'May I go back to work, Herr Stabsarzt? There is still much to do.' Brettschneider nodded curtly. I drew myself up to fullest attention, made a smart parade-ground right turn and marched left, right, left, right, for the door, which van Eck hastened to open. Outside I gave vent to my feelings. 'Bloody hun. Bloody man. Bloody farce. Pompous ass ...'

'It could have been worse,' van Eck said soothingly.

'I bet Webster wouldn't have kow-towed like that.'

'He would have if he had needed to to get his way. You have got yours, after all. The minimum waste of time considering everything and a happy Brettschneider who thinks he taught you to respect him.'

'I don't give a damn whether the sod's happy or miserable,' I said savagely.

'Ah but,' van Eck continued to soothe, 'a happy Brettschneider is best for all of us. You have really done us all a very good turn.'

At that my sense of humour was somehow reawakened and I started to laugh. 'You're a born diplomat van Eck. I'll have to recommend you for service in the Dutch Corps after the war.'

Back to work. The examination room was like a United Nations Social Club. My queue of British, Americans and Dutch hob-nobbed noisily with Denis' French, Belgians and Poles. My parachute insignia were a novelty to the patients, being the first that had been seen in Leipzig, and aroused frequent comment, the Battle of Arnhem becoming a convenient subject for the small talk that oils along the business of doctoring. I felt it incumbent upon me as the one and only British officer in the city, and with whom my compatriots there had any contact, to contribute all I could to the raising of morale. Although sorely pressed by the number of sick I was obliged to see and the constant nagging worry about making diagnostic mistakes I, therefore, made a point of trying to keep up the cheerful and confident front the occasion demanded. As is so often the case when immersed in something requiring 100 per cent concentration, time passed unnoticed. I never looked at my watch or even the big clock over the door until Denis tapped my shoulder, and said with a sympathetic smile,

'I have seen all my malades. Perhaps I can help you. You still have a number waiting and it grows late.'

It was a quarter past one and, allowing for the Brettschneider incident, I had worked non-stop for six hours – seven counting the ward round. So had Denis, and it was apparently nothing, the rule rather than the exception. I gratefully accepted his offer and together, after another half hour, we had cleared the room.

'Now we must eat,' Denis again smiled apologetically as if it were his fault, 'there are still the lager visits.'

Upstairs we waded into a meal the exact replica of breakfast. Denis asked me what had passed between the stabsarzt and myself.

'You tell him,' I said to van Eck, 'the thought of it spoils my food.'

Van Eck relayed the story, putting a gloss on it that gave me more credit than I felt was merited. If he had not been there I might have got myself into deep water, and sparked off a row having consequences beyond my own person. For Denis and the others emphatically agreed all had been for the best from the standpoint of the revier. Unless a major principle was involved, a serious difference of opinion concerning treatment of patients, a row was at all costs to be avoided. Brettschneider's position was a powerful one that enabled him to authorise or withold the benefits or, even, the necessities we might regard as deserving for the sick. Put him in a really bad mood and he was known to be capable of taking a savage delight in marking men fit for work, refusing special diets or taking other unpleasant measures out on them. Apart from snap visits, such as today, he routinely visited the revier twice a week to decide the disposal of special cases. It would be my task to present them to him if I thought, for example, a man's work should be changed, his rations increased or he had suffered some medical injustice. A German 'führer' in charge of a lager might query a case I had taken off work and send him up for Brettschneider's decision. He could be perfectly fair and reasonable. The important thing was to keep him well-humoured. This was something the Feldwebel also set much store by, he being, as it were, the buffer between ourselves and Brettschneider, and the first to feel his displeasure.

'But docility,' I objected, 'is not something the Parachute Corps encourages in the face of the enemy. Nor is it in my nature. My family would tell you that.'

'Do not think of it as docility,' said Denis, 'think of it as non-provocation. And now we must go, you to your lagers and I to mine.'

Down in his office the Feldwebel gave me the lager requests that had come in for visiting. They were at three different locations, fortunately in the same part of the city but a good distance from the revier. He gave van Eck the money needed for tram tickets and let us out through the front door. The sky was leaden and a few snowflakes were oscillating down through cold, windless air. We walked briskly along the pavements to a tram junction near the station, and had not long to wait before a 'train' of three single- decker tramcars, striking sparks from the overhead wire, and destined for our district, rattled to a stop. We boarded the front platform of the last coach.

'You must always travel on this platform. It is the rule for prisoners,' commented van Eck, 'we are not supposed to ride anywhere else. If it is very cold or wet the conductress may invite you inside, or you may ask her if there appears to be plenty of room. You could be roughly handled by other passengers if you otherwise break the rule.'

Van Eck bought the tickets, each with eight numbers on. No matter how far the journey only one number was punched, so that one Mark, the price of the card, bought eight journeys. The tram-train moved speedily and effectively through the city, passing areas reminiscent of London where piles of rubble testified to previous air-raids, and eventually we dismounted at a stop in a suburb, continuing the short remaining distance on foot.

The first place on the visiting list was a café commandeered and converted into a lock-up, barbed-wired lager for a British Commando, or working party, engaged in road mending. The main body of prisoners was still out at work, but in the Spartan living quarters were several miserable men confined to their bunks, two-tiered and closely packed as usual, with the lager sanitäte in attendance. Van Eck rousted him out of his cubby-hole and, having announced me by rank and name as the newly-arrived British doctor, called for the sick-book. I was fast realising how fortunate I was in having van Eck to ease my path. I had grossly overestimated my capacity to deal, in my crash-course German, with the ramifications of paper-work demanded by the job. Not only did I find it difficult immediately to grasp the essentials of the information recorded in the sick- book, but hard put to it to write down, as required, in German, my own findings, conclusions and recommendations. The result of my examination of each man, his diagnosis and treatment all had to go into the book, together with my decision as to his fitness for work. If unfit should he remain up and about in the lager on light duties, or stay in bed, or should he be transferred to the revier, or to one of the POW hospitals? Van Eck jotted all this down for me in double-quick time, while I made records in English for our own note-book which we carried round with us. We had selected this lager for our first visit as being the furthest from the revier. The next one was a short walk away where the men were confined in a more standard stone-built barrack hut, as found in the prison camps, situated adjacent to the gates and within the surrounding walls of a factory. Here, again, s everal sick men in double bunks had to be examined, sorted out and pre- scribed for. By now the afternoon was wearing on and twilight descend- ing. We hurried through the work intent on completing our mission and getting back to the revier, walking briskly on to the third lager which occupied the ground floor of what had once been a clothing store. The street would have once been busy with shoppers; now there were gaps in the buildings and a desolate air of down-at-heel abandonment, but the trams still ran the length of it, and we boarded one to make a connec- tion, at an intermediate junction, with that needed to take us back to the station.

At the junction we found ourselves caught up in a milling throng of Leipzigers and foreign workers, all competing for too few places in a scramble to get themselves home before blackout. It was the rush hour, all elbows and altercations. Seats went to the strongest. No courtesy toward women here. Several trams that would have done us stopped but were quickly filled, until the crowd had dwindled to a sprinkling of the elderly and ourselves. We had made attempts to board earlier, but the appropriate platform seemed always to be filled by others more practised at the flying jump by which this desirable eminence was most quickly gained. By the time we reached the station it was quite dark and snowing steadily. Van Eck produced a torch from his haversack, the beam restricted by a regulation blackout hood, and we picked our way towards the revier, footsteps muffled by the white mantle quickly form- ing on the ground as the temperature dropped below freezing point.

'Soon be home now.' Van Eck sounded cheerful.

'Home?' I said. 'I'll never be able to think of that Godforsaken work- house as home.'

'Perhaps you will, in time – it represents it for me. Friends, food and a place to sleep. important when you are tired and dispossessed.'

I was tired all right, and had to admit to myself I would be glad to turn the last corner into Gneisenau Strasse.

'Another good thing,' pursued van Eck, 'the snow.'

'Why the snow?' I was beginning to feel irritated at his effort to jolly me along, 'it'll only make getting around more difficult.'

'Oh no. The Germans will keep the trams running and the main side- walks constantly swept, they are used to it. No, the good part is we are unlikely to have our nights disturbed by air-raids. Once the snow season really sets in raids get fewer. The thicker the snow clouds the better for us.'

Even as we spoke the snow fall had sharpened into a blizzard, urged on by a freezing wind that found its way down our necks as we finally stood shivering outside the revier, waiting for the door to open to our ring. I had to be grateful I had a place to go, any port better than none. There were other prisoners, Russians especially, ill-clad and ill-housed, who suffered great privations during the bitter weather which proved to have set in for several weeks, and, as van Eck had predicted, it did feel good to step inside to the comparative warmth, even though the Feldwebel's welcome was somewhat frosty. We were his responsibility, and because of my inexpertise our visits had taken longer and we were much later than he expected. Van Eck, knowing our prolonged absence would have made him anxious, as much on his own behalf as ours, has- tened to explain the reason for our hold-up, to such good effect that the Feldwebel relaxed enough to give me a friendly pat on the back.'

'A long day Herr Doctor, nich var?'

It certainly had been but I was not finished just yet. Leaving our snow- covered overcoats with him for drying in the boiler room, we wearily climbed the stairs. I still had the evening round of the revier patients to make before putting my feet up. Denis had returned much earlier and was sitting at the table in our room writing a letter to his wife. He looked up as I came in.

'How does it go?!'

'It goes.'

I flopped into a chair and removed my boots, the same I had worn landing at Arnhem, now rather the worse for wear, and donned a pair of prisoner felt slippers I had acquired earlier on at Stalag 357.

'I must visit the sick, then I hope there will be something to eat.'

'Ready any time now,' Denis smiled, 'My wife is probably having a dish of fish with a white Burgundy. Even the Boches respected the vines. She tells me there has been a good gathering this year.'

'Really?' I did not smile and I knew within myself my answer was bleak. I felt bleak. Perhaps it was fatigue, but I did not find comparison of our circumstances with those of liberated France particularly congenial.

Poor Denis. He must have found me a churlish companion in the first few days, before I got my second wind and into the rhythm of working my long haul with the minimum waste of time and energy. Time saving meant cutting corners. If, for example, there were two hundred men to be seen at a morning sick parade and it took thirty seconds to move from one to the next it could cost me an hour and a half in extra time. Even fifteen seconds would cost three-quartes of an hour. The queue must be closed up, each man so hard on the heels of the one in front that I could move instantly from one to the other, without pause for introductory pleasantries. Pleasantries must accompany the examination but never precede it. Conservation of energy, I soon realised, depended on keeping very even tempered, never letting circumstances or people, especially Germans, like Brettschneider, provoke me. This was advice already received and I must take it. Emotion can be exhausting. Anger was a luxury I could not now afford, and never, but never must I allow myself to lie awake at night mulling over the day's encounters and thinking how I might have scored if I had only said so and so instead of this or that. Nor must I dwell at any time on the amount of work still waiting to be done. Sufficient unto the day? No. Sufficient unto the very minute was the task thereof.

The next morning, Saturday, it was still snowing hard. We were due to take a sick-parade at Hasag, on the outskirts of the city, and obliged to rise early, to leave the revier at 5 o'clock. David was in on this one, and the three of us shuffled off in the snow to a different tram stop, in the pitch dark, guided again by van Eck's torch. The streets were quite deserted until we came to a milk shop where a queue of women had already gathered. We heard their voices before we saw them, twittering animatedly even at this early hour. Van Eck said we would always find them there, no matter the weather or night disturbance from air-raid warnings. The women of Leipzig, save those with very young children or the very elderly, were all employed on war work or essential services of some kind, and were obliged to get their shopping done before their shifts started. Even the old and frail could not afford to miss whatever was going by delaying until a more civilised hour, and they too were there, braving the cold, waiting with patient resignation for their turn and lugging their purchases home behind them in little four-wheeled miniature carts.

At this hour there were not so many people lining up for the trams and we were able to take seats inside the rear compartment. The journey and all the subsequent ones afforded me much interest. One never knew with whom one might rub shoulders, and there were many ready to strike up a conversation, especially foreign workers who, Russians excepted, were often indistinguishable from the home-grown civilians. Russians, easily recognised by the poverty of their clothing and pinched faces, were seen as objects of abhorrence. Notwithstanding it was Nazi policy to keep them looking ragged and wolfish in order to impress on all citizens the necessity of preventing the country from being overrun by these hordes, and notwithstanding the fact this policy was well known, it worked. The man in the street looked upon them and was stiffened in his resolve to persist in his war effort, despite the bleak military news he had for so many months been obliged to digest. In more than one conversation I was asked why we British could not recognise a common interest between ourselves and Germany in saving Europe from the communists. We should be combining, not fighting, was the oft-repeated theme. I refused to be drawn. 'Avoid politics like the plague,' Webster had told me. 'You can't tell who is a fanatic and who isn't until you're too far in to get out, and if you get on the wrong side of a fanatic you could be in trouble.'

The conductress on this morning's run turned out to be a Dutch woman, well known to van Eck and probably why we were favoured with a seat. I chanced a pleasantry or two, thinking to make my number with her for future journeys, and was surprised by the warmth of her response. She was a German national by marriage, her husband lost on the eastern front, and after a quick look round to make sure we were not overheard said she was sorry we, the British, had lost the battle at Arnhem, as the one and only thing she was looking forward to was to see the Allies marching into Leipzig, from the west.

Unfortunately for us the number of passengers soon increased and at this early hour were not in the best of tempers. An armed soldier, a burly corporal, got in at one stop and sat down opposite. Van Eck and David had already moved to make way for civilians, and I was the only one of our group still seated. I was feeling rather drowsy, a combination of the early hour and comparative warmth of the compartment, and paying little attention to what was going on around me. But, glancing idly in the direction of the corporal, I became very much aware that he was eyeing me balefully, and of an uncomfortable current of hostility flowing towards me from his direction. Suddenly, slinging his rifle, he got up and advanced on me, seized me by the lapels of my overcoat, yanked me roughly to my feet and shouted coarsely,

'Aufstehen. Heraus. Get up. Out onto the platform. Swinehound.' Still holding me by the lapels he started to shake me like a terrier with a rat, and to pull me in the direction of the door. It was more than I could take. All my good resolutions about keeping even tempered went by the board, and I started shouting back, fuelling my feelings of outrage with the sound of my own strident voice.

'Ich bin offizier. I am an officer. You have no right to touch me.' I pointed to the pips on my shoulder and the Red Cross armband 'Ich bin stabsarzt. Stabsarzt verstehen sie? Und du bist nur Gefreite. Take your filthy hands off me. Gehen sie zurück. I will report you to my headquarters. Geben mir dein name bitte. Dein verhalten ist nich Korrekt. Take your hands off me. Sofort. Sofort. Nich Korrekt.'

I glared at him, eyeball to eyeball, seething with indignation, but I had the good sense to keep my hands to myself. The atmosphere was touch and go. The other passengers were looking on, impassive and silent. And then one said 'nich korrekt', and then another, and the gefreite looked around him and faltered. I felt his grip slacken and then he dropped his arms. I said to van Eck and David, who had been standing anxiously by, 'Better go out onto the platform.' They nodded. I gave the gefreite another glare, turned my back on him and made for the door. 'Bloody hun,' I was still seething. How dare he handle me? It was an affront to my uniform. But I had learned something. Rank definitely counted. David and van Eck were looking at me now we were safely outside with expressions on their faces I could only interpret as approval mingled with relief. I had repelled an enemy boarder; simply by reacting in the way natural to me – an Englishman, as bloody-minded as any beneath the surface. It might have been more dignified to have remained calm and icily soft-spoken but would it have been more effective? Who knows? Van Eck said the trouble was my red beret. At the time of Arnhem the German radio and press had, after the issue was decided, declared that prisoners wearing airborne insignia should be regarded as potential trouble makers, only a degree removed from criminals. The beret could have been like a red rag to a bull. So be it. I had no intention of wearing anything else.

At Hasag was one of the bigger lagers, the focal point for several smaller satellites, and here I took a sick parade very much after the pattern of yesterday's at the revier, only, thankfully, much fewer in number. I paid more attention to the clock, pacing myself according to my rate of progress, and put into effect the queue-bunching ploy to save the precious seconds between patients. I also had David interviewing them before they reached me, so that they could be stripping off in advance, and exposing the portions of their anatomy indicated as the seat of their trouble ready for my examination. Having seen off the German gefreite in the tram I was now feeling pleased with myself and jovial; on top of things for the first time since arriving in Leipzig. I judged the sick parade a success; plenty of good humoured banter with the men, no diagnostic mistakes that I was aware of, good rapport established on my first visit, and all finished in good time to make it back to the revier for a decent lunch break. Van Eck judged it otherwise.

'You went well over the limit with the off-works. Nearly twenty percent.'

'I was feeling generous.'

'I did warn you.'

'Perhaps it won't be noticed.'

'I should not count on it.'

'Well I thought they were all deserving cases.'

'So you said. But Brettschneider may not think so.'

'To hell with Brettschneider.' I had become too buoyant to heed van Eck, who had indeed warned me when I had reached the ten-per-cent cut off point. Ten-per-cent had been a figure others in my game had impressed upon me as being the allowable upper limit. I had never had it spelt out to me by the Germans themselves in so many words. Well, we would see. It had stopped snowing, the sun was now shining, the city sparkling like a Christmas tree, the journey back to the revier uneventful, and I was in fine fettle. Even the Feldwebel had good news for me.

'There have been no requests in for visits this afternoon. You are free to go out. Van Eck will take you to the public baths. Next time you will know the proceedure and can go on your own.'

Van Eck explained it was customary for the staff of the revier to try to get to the baths once a week. They were open daily and it was more often than not the occupation of a Sunday morning. But an available Saturday afternoon was better as it left the whole of Sunday free for other things; visiting colleagues in the POW hospitals and one's patients who may be in there, taking a constitutional, doing a bit of shopping, shaving soap and the like, buying a drink at a bar, savouring what little there was left of civilisation in an historic city forever associated with the name of Johann Sebastian Bach, who worked here from 1723 until his death in 1750.

At the public baths we bought for one Mark a ticket giving us access to the shower-house. It was spotlessly clean, every cubicle lined with gleaming white tiles. A warm towel was thrown in with the ticket, brought to us by a female attendant who also provided a well-used bar of ersatz soap, faintly redolant of Eau-de-Cologne. The water was piping hot, and it was a luxurious pleasure to feel thoroughly sudded after days of contact with none too sanitary prisoners. All the travelling and show-ering was paid by the Germans, but there was never any problem about money needed for by our own personal purchases and amusements. As long as there were parcels and cigarettes we had the currency that counted. Van Eck had contacts and ran the bank. He was also the agent for the supply of forbidden items, films for the camera, new valves for the wireless set, and it was said, but never openly discussed, the link man with organisations who could, at a price, set up an escape, providing all the necessary papers, clothes and cover-stories for a bold-as-brass walk onto a train in broad daylight in Leipzig station.

On returning to the revier and reporting to the Feldwebel we found him in an uncommonly good humour, you might say cock-a-hoop. The

German radio, he hastened to inform us, his battered old face crinkled in glee, had announced the launching of a massive attack against the Americans in the Ardennes. In what was being described as an unprecedented counter-offensive designed to win the war in the West, eight Panzer divisions were already smashing forward along the chosen front and destroying the myth of invincibilty of the Allied armies. I was sceptical.

'Eight Panzer divisions. Is that so?'

'Ja wohl. You will see. They will cut your armies in half and then destroy them.'

I was vague about the actual territorial dispositions of the Allied forces at this time, there had been few reports of movement recently on the BBC, and found his news disquieting, but I wasn't going to let him put me down.

'Oh well,' I said, 'the Russians will be glad not to be having those Panzers opposing them. It would not surprise me if the Americans left the door open deliberately to entice them in. And after they are in they will close it,' I opened my hand and then made it into a fist, 'like this.'

Had Denis and the others heard the news? They had, and we were all agreed that judgement should be suspended until we had the BBC report. The evening bulletin confirmed the attack, but did not say much and was short on detail.

'That country is not good for tanks, I have been there,' commented Denis, 'but good for defence. Me, I cannot think it will amount to much.'

Van Eck was the most worried. 'Do not underestimate them. Look what happened at Arnhem. They are still formidable. If they should reach the sea you British will be cut off from your supplies. You could find yourselves being squeezed from north and south and Holland.' He sounded most unhappy, 'Holland could once again all be in their hands.'

I could well see the force of his argument and why such an outcome would cause him despair, and his words affected me, evoking a sympathetic reaction of foreboding. After all I had been part of an élite force that had descended upon Arnhem as confident liberators and left it as despondent vanquished – those that were still alive. I could say nothing to van Eck. But Denis kept our spirits up.

'All the same. Think of all the Allied forces in the south, and how the Germans are overstretched on two fronts. I do not believe they can succeed. If the Allies found it possible to land from the sea in Normandy, and build up, and break out when all the advantages were with the Boches, they can surely hold a counter-attack in circumstances most suited to themselves?'

That made sense and we all nodded. Denis was the oldest in our group and had made his career in the French Army, as a doctor. He went on,

'The vital factor is the Allied air power. I tell you the Boche will not succeed.'

I felt, as one of the members of the inevitably victorious Allied armies I was, perhaps, making a rather poor showing at this juncture and should reinforce Denis' confident attitude; for my own, I was coming to realise, like it or not and despite my relative youth, could have a direct effect on our communal morale. It might seem disproportionate but it saddled me with a kind of ambassadorial accountability. Not only must I never let the enemy see me dispirited, but never, either, my fellow prisoners. So I said,

'Denis is absolutely right. The Allies have total mastery of the air. We shall inevitably defeat them.' Then for good measure I added 'but the Feldwebel is happy. And if the Feldwebel is happy that is good news for us anyway. Ha, ha!'

Ha, ha. The little group dissolved and went about its individual business. Denis and I took to our room, where I applied myself to my German studies while he got out his top boots and began to polish them.

'You look as if you are preparing for a general's inspection, I bantered.'

He held the boot, into which his left hand was plunged, up to the light and flashed me a smile. 'C'est bon ça. N'est ce pas? No, I would not take all this trouble for a mere general. It is for the promenade tomorrow. Bretiot is coming over. We always take a stroll the Sunday mornings. I hope you will join us. We then take déjeuner here, and in the afternoon visit the hospital where Bretiot works. You will meet many new colleagues.'

'Thank you,' I said, 'it will give me much pleasure.' Then a new thought struck me. 'It is nearly Christmas you know. Will we be doing anything special?'

'The Boches will. The Feldwebel will get drunk and tell us how he admires the British and French, and give us a few bottles of wine.'

'Stolen from France?'

'Very likely. We shall have a cake and candles, listen to Christmas songs on the German radio, sing a few ourselves, and the next day it will be back to normal, only worse because the Feldwebel will have a hangover.'

I went to sleep thinking of Christmases past before the Nazis' lust for power had disrupted the world, then of the offensive in the Ardennes. It must not succeed.

Sunday dawned dry and sparkling. Denis dressed himself in his number one uniform; immaculate riding breeches, gleaming top-boots, beautifully cut tunic, and kepi at a slightly rakish angle. I felt very scruffy, still wearing the battle-dress I had landed in. True, it had had a brush-up and press by the tut-tutting mess orderly at Stalag 357, but I feared I cut a sorry sartorial figure in comparison, especially when Bretiot arrived, not quite as immaculate as Denis but very smart nevertheless. My great consolation was my red beret, the only one in Leipzig of which I was aware. No need to feel inferior to anyone with that on my head.

We stepped out into the sunlight where Denis paused on the steps of the revier, and glanced up and across to the apartment block opposite. Some net curtains twitched slightly, then a window opened and a girl with red hair put her head out, looked quickly up and down Gneisenau Strasse and waved. Denis saluted and blew her a kiss, which she returned. Then abruptly she withdrew her head, shut the window and closed the curtains, and it was as if nothing had happened.

'Ah. Ma belle Lili,' sighed Denis, 'one of these days we shall meet.'

'How do you know her name is Lili?' I asked, mightily intrigued.

'I do not know it,' Denis replied, still gazing towards the window as we set off down the road, 'but I do know she wants me as much as I want her.'

Bretiot took his arm. 'Perhaps it can be arranged, but not today Henri. There are other girls in Leipzig you know.'

'There is no other girl in Leipzig so desirable,' Denis said emphatically, 'and she is so near.'

'And yet so far.' Bretiot increased his pace, 'come on, Henri, let us inspect the rest of the field.'

And that is what the promenade turned out to be. Two jaunty French officers boldly eyeing all the ladies in sight, even crossing the road to obtain a closer view if one took their fancy; while I tagged along, not exactly disinterested, that would be to misstate my sexual orientation, but tired, jaded after the recent days' hard work and unable to see the point of it all. Why excite oneself when there was no prospect of fulfilment? For a German to talk to a prisoner of war in public was an offence punishable by at least two years in prison. A girl who had intercourse with a prisoner committed an offence punishable by death, while for the prisoners, at the very least, there were the correction camps like Falingbostel.

We strolled towards the centre of the city, an area known as the Ring, once the centre of the European fur trade. Now, after having been devastated by RAF fire-bomb raids, it was a desolate shell of its former self, a mart only for rabbit skins. But there were a few shops and cafés still functioning, and my French companions entered one of the latter without hesitation, descending some stone steps to a large Bier-Keller to which, it seemed to me in retrospect, they had set an unerring compass course from the very start. It was all very noisy and animated, and we sat down at a table some distance from the servery bar in what was, patently, the peak hour of the Sunday morning business. I felt very uncomfortable, as though the eyes of every German in the place must be upon us. After all how would a crowd of Londoners have reacted if a German officer had come and sat down with two Italian officers in the Lyons Corner house off Piccadilly Circus. Perhaps they would not have been distinguished from all the different uniforms always seen round that area. At any rate Denis and Bretiot were quite unconcerned, and continued to carry out their exercise of looking around and trying to catch the eyes of the girls. As nothing happened I began to relax, and then a waitress came up to to the table full of smiles for Denis and Bretiot.

'Bon jours mes amis,' she cried, 'mais,' and here she looked boldly at me, 'Je n'ai pas fait la connaissance de cet officier.'

Denis introduced me with many a flourishing gesture, and to my intense embarrassment she sat herself down beside me, and started telling me her family history – in English. She had married a man from Blackpool, wandered all over Europe with him before the war, finally left him and, finding herself in Leipzig when the war broke out, had got herself a job here and held it ever since. As I listened I looked at the adjacent tables; surely some German would find this fraternising offensive to him. I was on the point of deciding I had better walk out when something more embarrassing, unbelievably embarrassing, happened. She beckoned another waitress, who came over, and said to her excitedly, again in English,

'Gretel, your chance has come at last, here is a captain, a doctor, not long ago left England.'

Gretel, who was no lightweight, thereupon placed herself firmly on my lap, flung her arms passionately round my neck and implored me to take her to England with me after the war was over. I was speechless, totally nonplussed, and looked helplessly at Denis, hoping he would do something to extricate me. My silence was the signal for another outburst from Gretel.

'If you did not want me yourself,' she cried, clasping me even more tightly, 'I would gladly offer to become Churchill's chambermaid.'

This was too much for me. I was scared stiff. She must be mad and would get us all arrested. I prised her arms off my neck, stood up abruptly, causing her to totter and nearly fall, and staring straight ahead left the premises as fast as I could, expecting every second to feel a

German hand to come up from behind and clamp my shoulder. Denis and Bretiot must have found this turn events also too much for them, as they quickly followed me out. We had not even ordered, let alone had a drink, and I feared I would be reproached for having spoiled their morning. Far from it. They were looking at me in admiration.

'What a Don Juan.'

'A veritable hit with the girls.'

'Tell us your secret' And so on. I smiled sheepishly.

'I expect it was my shaving soap. But seriously, it must not happen again, it is very dangerous is it not?'

'Yes,' said Denis, 'it is very dangerous – in theory. But you know the saying, eat drink and be merry for tomorrow we die? That is how the Leipzigers look at life. They do not bother too much about the rules.'

I looked at Bretiot for confirrnation

'That is true. But we have to watch out for those in uniform, and for the Gestapo, although they know we are in a special category by our Red Cross brassards.'

'All the same,' I said, 'I am not going in there again. Is there not somewhere else we can go where we are not likely to attract so much attention?'

'Oui. Bien sur.'

Denis and Bretiot led me off in another direction and we fetched up at a smaller cafe, much less boisterous in atmosphere, with an older clientele, where we sat down once again, giving our order to a poker-faced waitress who scarcely threw us a nod. Denis and Bretiot took a glass of white wine while I had a Stein of Helle Bier. The conversation at adjacent tables, easily overheard since the Leipzigers seemed to speak in naturally loud voices, was all on the subject of the Ardennes offensive, and I gathered it was thought to be going well for the Germans. Denis and Bretiot had lost their previous animation, due I surmised to a lack of pretty faces in the cafe; and after a second round of drinks suggested it was time to return to the revier.

On the way we passed a bookshop where one or two English titles in the window display caught my attention.

'A moment,' I begged the others, 'I would rather like to look inside if it is OK.'

'Why not,' said Denis, 'it is open.'

I scanned the shelves. Books in English were few and far between and mostly classics, Dickens and the like. Recent publications were of the pre-war pro-fascist variety. But I seized on a novel, 'This above all?' by Eric Knight, attracted by the quotation from Polonius' speech in Hamlet, and purchased it for a few marks. Reading it later I discovered its hero was a conscientious objector, not that I in any way looked down on the taking up of such a stance. I was a non-combatant, automatically spared the necessity of killing, and thus of taking a decision of his kind. But I had no doubt, had I not been a doctor looking upon the war as I did as a necessary evil, a lesser evil than the occupation of the British Isles by an enemy, pagan power, and the exposure of our inhabitants, woman and children not exempted, to the same brutalities and horrors that had been suffered on the mainland, I would have killed Germans without compunction on the 'us or them' basis. No, my regret at the theme of this very good book was the the lesson of the bookshop. The only recent publications on sale from Britain were totally unrepresentative of the mainstream of opinion and outlook, and served merely to bolster Nazi propaganda to the effect we were fighting the war against our will through the machinations of international Jewry. This was a constant theme of Goebbles' radio, coupled with British blindness in not recognising the Russian menace to European civilisation. It was always conveniently forgotten that the Nazis had first invaded and trampled western Europe under the heels of their jackboots, committed frightful atrocities and then, having failed by a whisker to subdue the British Isles, turned their ambitious wrath against Russia, with whom they had signed a pact of alliance. Now they were afraid, and rightly so. They were losing to the Russians, who could be expected to exact a terrible retribution for the frightfulness they had experienced at German hands. In their broadcasts the Nazis encouraged a twin strand of wishful thinking in their listeners; the infallibility of Hitler and his secret weapons to come, and the belief that the West would, at the eleventh hour, join with them in opposing the Russian advances.

A not inconsiderable number of prisoners with whom I came in contact had absorbed this propaganda, and believed it to a greater or lesser extent. It was difficult not to be touched by it in a place like Leipzig, where prisoners of so many nationalities lived lives not so very different from the indigent civilians. But I never bought it. I was too fresh from home. The questions that took priority in my mind were whether the Germans would give up before the Russians or Americans (we were on the axis of advance of the American First Army) reached Leipzig; if they did not give up who would get here first; and if it looked like being the Russians which would be my better option, allow myself to be liberated by them or try to escape westwards?

After what Denis was pleased to call le dejeuner, thin potato soup with bread and sausage, we went by train to Bretiot's POW hospital in the suburb of Warhen. Here was the first establishment I had seen since entering Germany that remotely approached the standards I had been used to at home. There was a lack of sophisticated medicines, but real medical expertise was available in the persons of the resident doctors and surgeons. The senior doctor was a charming Yugoslavian whose gifts of kindness and tact welded the medical staff of many nationalities, French, Italian, Dutch and even Indian, into an effective and cooperative team. The wards were airy, with adequate spacing between the beds, nursing (all male) was good, sanitary arrangements satisfactory, and the food was as good as could be expected within the framework of the general shortages in Leipzig.

I went round the wards visiting the patients who came from my 'practice'. Apart from serious injuries sustained at work, those under treatment were mostly suffering from chest infections or peptic ulcers. Ulcers were particularly prevalent, stemming from the rough rations and stressful living to which lager prisoners were exposed. But a high incidence of peptic ulceration was by no means confined to prisoners of war. The German army had serious problems with this condition, and to facilitate management of diet and medication had formed 'Ulcer Battalions', rear line units supposedly only fit for light duties, but which, in the end, found themselves in the front line fighting alongside the élite.

We bade farewell to Bretiot and made our way back to the revier. Denis remarked on the clear starlit night and remarked this might mean Allied bomber incursions into Germany later on. He was right. We were obliged to stand-to twice on reports of 'enemy formations approaching our zone'. He explained to me the significance of the map of the Reich with the superimposed grid formation, in the Feldwebels office, dividing the country into zones. The German radio broadcast the plotted course of the raiders zone by zone so the Feldwebel could tell at a glance the direction in which the attack was developing, and estimate our chances of being included in the target area. It was very tiresome having to get up in the night preparatory to a possible descent to the cellar, but we consoled ourselves with the knowledge that the Feldwebel and his staff were as equally put out, if not more so. It was their country taking the beating.

The next day, Monday, was a repetition of Friday; a huge sick-parade in the morning, with visits to lagers in the afternoon. Tuesday was Hasag again in the morning with more lager visits later, Wednesday a repeat of Monday, Thursday of Tuesday, and suddenly I realised I had been in Leipzig a week – only a week. It felt like a lifetime. As if to mark the occasion the birds of my first visit to Hasag, when van Eck had warned me I had been over-generous with my off-work certificates, came home to roost. The Lager had informed Brettschneider, who put in an unheralded appearance there on the Thursday movning. Remembering our previous encounter, and not knowing at first what had prompted his visit, I greeted him politely and correctly.

'Good morning, Herr Stabsarzt,' I stood to attention and looked him straight in the face, 'I hope you are well.'

His beady eyes glinted behind his glasses. 'As well as many of the men you have been letting off work.'

'Oh?'

'You are not severe enough with your men. You have been letting them off for trivialities. A German soldier would be fighting at the front with the same complaints you send your men to rest for.'

This, of course was true. Any man in Germany was thrown into the fight unless he was blind, or a hopeless cripple, or in a reserved occupation. But I really could not abide Brettschneider and, despite all the good advice I had received, I began to feel combative. His remarks were really an admission of the weakness of the German military position.

'Excuse me please, Herr Stabsarzt,' I tried to keep my voice calm and level, 'but the standards I have been working to are the same as those we apply to the very numerous German prisoners of war in England,' I stressed the 'very numerous', 'would you want us to be more severe with them?'

I stole a quick glance at van Eck, who was beginning to look anxious, but I thought to myself I was taking a pretty good line of argument, even that I might have him there. But I hadn't. He remained silent only for a moment, while I stood with my hands behind my back in the classical non-provocative posture.

'I know nothing about the treatment of German prisoners in England,' he said icily, 'and I would remind you we are not *in* England. We are in Germany. And you, a prisoner of the German army, will conform to the procedures of the German army. Do you understand? Please proceed with your work.'

'Jawohl, Herr Stabsarzt.'

Further argument was useless. He was obviously intending to remain and supervise my sick-parade. I would have to fight the cases with him if and when the need arose. This exchange had taken place while the head of the sick queue, already in the room, were well within earshot. As I beckoned the next man forward a good deal of muttering started, that spread rearwards like a fuse. David told me afterwards the men had approved my stand and understood my dilemma. To my question, 'do you feel well enough to work', the no's were all entirely genuine. Brettschneider was given no opportunity to catch me out signing off malingerers. They would bide their time for a more propitious occasion. By the end of the morning he had thawed.

115

'You have been very correct today. I appreciate your cooperation. I hope it will continue. Auf wiedersehen.'

'Auf wiedersehen Herr Stabsarzt, und Vielen Dank.'

I did not know which I disliked most, his hectoring or his praise. But it was really no thanks to me we had parted on good terms. It was entirely owing to the prisoners, who had let me off the hook by restraining their requests for relief.

Friday was another grinding day, but on Saturday, on my return from Hasag, the Feldwebel had a pleasant surprise in store.

'You are in luck. There is a Christmas party at Oschatz, and you have permission to attend. Be ready to leave after Mittagessen. You will return here tomorrow.' This was indeed a piece of welcome news. A change of scene, if only for a day, would I knew do my morale good. Moreover I might be able to find out more about what was happening in the Ardennes. We continued to be worried as the German radio was jubilant at the rate of progress they claimed to be making while the BBC broadcasts we were able to pick up were not saying much.

'I certainly am in luck, Feldwebel …' then a thought struck me, 'might there possibly be time for me to visit the public baths before I go?' I had been looking forward to it all the week.

The Feldwebel looked at his watch and consulted a train time-table.

'Yes. If you are very quick.'

'And my patients here?'

'Stabsarzt Denis has agreed to look after them.'

I bounded up the stairs two at a time, and finding Denis already started on his meal, joined him at the table and tucked in, thanking him between mouthfuls for taking on my work and briefing him on the cases, and what I had in mind for their treatment. Then I took myself off to the baths, had my longed-for shower, and was back in the revier before 3pm. I was on the train three-quarters of an hour later, escorted by one of the private soldiers from the revier, and once again in the padre's quarters at Oschatz soon after half past five.

'Very glad to see you again,' he welcomed me.

'And you too.'

'I thought you might be glad of a little light relief from Leipzig, and managed to persuade the Chefarzt to give you leave.'

'That was very good of you.'

'It was nothing. By the way, you are C of E aren't you?'

'Why, yes.'

'A communicant?'

I felt myself blushing. 'Very intermittently I am afraid.'

'Christmas?'

'I try not to miss.'

'You have to be back in the revier tomorrow.'

'So I understand.'

'Would you like a service now? We have time before the show.'

I was the sort of self-conscious person who, when it came to the most intimate liturgical expression of the faith I professed, such as it was, preferred to participate and get lost in a crowd. I began to prevaricate.

'Isn't that putting you to an awful lot of trouble?'

'No more trouble to me, than for you to see a patient,' then, after a pause, 'would you like me to hear your confession first?'

This really panicked me.

'I haven't been used to that.' I remembered how, as a schoolboy being prepared for confirmation, the parson at the end of the course of instruction had asked me the same question and frightened me out of my wits. 'N-no thank you sir,' I had mumbled, seeing in front of me not a parson but a policeman. He had given me a penetrating stare. 'Well, my boy. Do not forget. If ever you think you have done something wrong you can be sure you will have, and you must lose no time in confessing it to God. He knows all and hears all!' 'I will sir. I will. I promise I will.' I would have promised anything to escape from those X-ray eyes. Now the eyes that looked at me, although reminiscent of those others, were themselves anxious, and their owner was saying in an understanding voice,

'That is entirely for you to say. Your churchmanship is your business. But the service?'

I gave up. Why not? 'Yes. Yes padre. It is very good of you.' And as soon as I had said it my reservations seemed to melt away from me and I felt a kind of liberation. It was all right. Right for me, and I wanted it.

'Almighty God unto whom all hearts be open, all desires known and from whom no secrets are hid, cleanse ...'

The show put on by the camp was an astonishing pantomime, a remarkable mixture of Cinderella, Snow White, Dick Whittington and Alladin, in which the characters were recognisable by their costumes but the dialogue bore no relation to traditional themes. It was sheer improvisation, a pot-pourri of slapstick sketches and popular songs, heroes and heroines patently identifiable to those in the audience as take-offs of members of their camp, villains blatantly obvious as the Camp Commandant and his staff. But not obvious to them. The Commandant was in the front row of the audience, and, many German guards were dotted about the concert hall. All without exception stared uncomprehendingly at the spectacle before them, wearing expressions of blank amazement, failing completely to see in the grotesque antics of the ugly

117

sisters any reference to themselves, or in a dance routine with high-kicks a hilarious send-up of the goose step.

The padre having been very much involved in the production asked me to join him on the stage at the end. 'Say a few words of cheer, you are the most recently out from home. They would appreciate it.'

I hammered away at the theme of our invincibility, at the tremendous progress we had made since D-day. I said the Gennans in the Ardennes were putting their heads into a prepared noose, and I had no doubt we should all be home before the summer. These sentiments were predictably greeted by prolonged applause. The Commandant looked sour. But not as sour as when the pianist struck up the opening bars of Land of Hope and Glory, the audience rose as one man and, with the cast assembled on the stage, sang their heads off in a most moving expression of national fervour, highlighted by the slow lowering of a prisoner-made portrait of King George VI and Queen Elizabeth from the flies to the level of the heads of those on the stage.

Later, in the padre's room I broached the topic of the Ardennes.

'You get round the camps, padre, have you any hard news of what is really happening out there?'

'The general consensus is the Yanks have been caught with their pants down. Jerry has penetrated some distance and there has been quite a flap on. But nobody doubts the situation will be restored. In fact on yesterday's news there was a hint they may have stopped advancing, but one doesn't know for sure.'

'I feel very cut off at Leipzig. It's a strange atmosphere, everyone waiting. Germans pretending they're winning the war. Prisoners very uneasy. They know there's going to be a big squeeze and if the Germans put up strong resistance in the city there might be another Stalingrad-type battle, with them in the middle – if they haven't been marched off somewhere else first. It's rumoured the Germans are herding all prisoners out of the path of the Russians.'

'We've heard that too.'

I changed the subject. 'Have you any news of Webster at Naunhof?'

'He's OK now. He did a long stint at Leipzig and got very run down. The Chefarzt uses Naunhof as a rehabilitation centre for overworked MOs or, as in your case, for probationary assessment. Don't forget if you ever feel you must have a change from Leipzig you can always apply to the Chefarzt for a transfer.'

'I can't say I've ever worked such long hours or carried so much responsibility. I get tired but I'll be all right. It's an education really.'

'That's the best way to look at it.' The padre held my eyes. 'You know, everything in life has a meaning. What we are doing at any given time

118

can undoubtedly be a significant preparation for something else – if we use it well.

My visit to Oschatz did me a world of good, thanks mainly to the padre. I went round with him in the morning, visiting various barrack huts, enjoying cups of coffee or tea and a cheerful chat, and he gave me a slap-up food-parcel midday meal to fortify me for the journey back to the revier. Before leaving I was interviewd by the Chefarzt. He didn't say much, merely expressed the hope that I was settling down in Leipzig, and wouldn't be faced with much winter sickness. I ventured to suggest another pair of medical hands would not go amiss. But he looked blank and that was all.

It was Christmas Eve, and at the revier preparations were in full swing for the next day's feast. By pooling resources and a bit of under-the-counter bartering we had mustered a good supply of beer, enough Spam for a blow-out of fritters, and a stack of chocolate bars. Petit had 'found' the ingredients to make a large cake, with icing, and Denis had hoarded his wife's last parcel of nuts and dried fruit. All we lacked were presents.

'Couldn't we find something to put in the poor old Feldwebel's stocking –' I suggested. Denis wrinkled his nose.

'You would not be able to find a volunteer to get near enough. Anyway,' van Eck grinned, 'he never hangs up his stockings. He stands them up beside his boots – if he hasn't gone to bed in them.'

The Feldwebel was always good as a butt for jokes amongst ourselves, and I was about to keep the ball rolling when David, who had slipped away hoping to raise the BBC on our rather temperamental radio, burst into the room waving a bit of paper.

'It looks as if the Gemans in the Ardennes have run out of steam,' he cried pointing to the note he had made, 'the BBC are saying they have definitely been stopped, and that our own counter-offensive is under way.'

Someone raised a cheer. 'Hold on a minute' I said, 'what are the Germans saying?'

'They're talking about regrouping.'

'Ties in with what the padre told me. Looks good.' After my experiences at Arnhem I had become so wary of wishful thinking I did not like to give public vent to my private feelings, high though they were, at this ostensibly authentic news. Not so the others. The French embraced each other, slapped me on the back and, despite myself, sucked me into their mood of uninhibited celebration as they started pouring out the beer.

'Save some for Christmas!' I tried to protest.

'Oh, never mind. We'll get some more. Come on,' Denis raised his mug, 'here's to the Allies and victory. Santé.'

119

'Santé.'

'C'est ça alors. Their last throw. The war is as good as finished.'

I did not want to put a damper on the occasion and made no comment. But I was thinking, the reality is we still have to drive them back to their starting point, deal with the Siegfried line and cross the Rhine, too early to count the chickens. Nevertheless, the news was very welcome, and with the night being overcast, snow-filled and air-raid free, and myself full of beer, I enjoyed a deep, untroubled sleep, until roused by the Feldwebel at half-past five on Christmas morning.

'Aufstehen captain. You must get up.' He was shaking me by the shoulder.

I grumbled loudly. 'Why so early? On Christmas Day. You said it was to be like a Sunday.'

'There is an urgent request for a visit from one of the American lagers.'

Oh lord, I thought, what now.

'Van Eck is getting ready. Leave as soon as you can.'

'Will the trains be running today?'

'Of course. Why not?'

'Well if I must I must. Some breakfast first?'

'Ja Wohl, aber schnell.'

Van Eck and I set off. There was a thick carpet of snow, but gangs of prisoner-workers had already been busy and were in process of clearing the tram lines, while citizens were gathered in their usual queues at the dairies. As it became lighter curtains were drawn, and Christmas trees could be seen in some of the windows. It was a grey day and very cold. Fortunately the tram was empty enough for us to take refuge inside.

The American lager, to which I had previously paid one short visit, there being relatively few prisoners for the accommodation available, with, consequently, less in the way of contact illnesses, now resembled the black hole of Calcutta. Every available bunk was occupied and dejected men were sitting about on the floor, the very picture of misery. Van Eck spoke briefly to the Lagerführer and then turned to me.

'These are new arrivals. Came in last night. Prisoners taken in the Ardennes.' Bloody Ardennes, Were we never to be given the chance to think of something else. I raised my voice above the level of continuous mutterings and groans.

'May I speak to the senior soldier of the new intake please?!'

A man detached himself from a huddled group and stepped forward.

'Tell me your problems.'

120

'You a medic?'

I explained who I was.

'These guys are all dead beat. Some have frost—bite. Most have dysentery ...'

'You mean real dysentery or just diarrhoea?'

'I wouldn't know, but they need to go to the john every five minutes.'

The smell coming from numerous buckets was evidence enough of that. I looked around, realising I would have to make a thorough examination of every single one of them, at least fifty in all. It was obvious there would be cases for the hospital and a need for ambulances. I turned to van Eck.

'Get Brettschneider down here.'

'On Christmas Day?'

'I don't care what day it is. Get him.'

Van Eck went off to the Lagerführer's office to telephone and I went to work. It was the worst situation I had been confronted with since Falingbostel. Many of the men were in a very poor way indeed, shocked, emaciated, dehydrated and hypothermic. I gave my first attention to those lying inertly in bunks looking really ill, and soon had several case sheets completed of undoubted hospital cases. Van Eck raised the Feldwebel on the telephone and managed to persuade him, albeit reluctantly, to contact Brettechneider.

'Is he coming?'

'Feldwebel will let us know.'

'When?'

'He did not say.'

'Is it possible to connect me direct to Brettschneider?'

'I can try.'

'Please do so.'

Van Eck once again disappeared into the office, to emerge some minutes later with a different look on his face.

'Brettschneider is on his way.'

'Thanks for that.'

I never thought there would be a time when I would be glad to see him, but his arrival was an unqualified relief. He huffed and puffed at first, suspicious I might have got him out on false pretences, but as soon as I had shown him the case sheets and the men to whom they referred he became brisk, and efficiently professional.

'You are right stabsarzt, these men must be taken to Wahren. I will arrange it forthwith.'

There were only two ambulances available in Leipzig for POW transport, but he had them both at the lager within the half hour; by which time he had donned a white coat, slung a stethoscope round his neck and joined me in the examination of the patients, with van Eck attached to him as interpreter. Half way through the morning he called me aside.

'Wahren is full. They cannot take any more. How many free places have you at Gneisenau Strasse?'

'There were four last night.'

'Not enough. We must use this lager as a relief revier, and you must visit it daily. I will send two sanitätes and a supply of kaoli and morphia. I would expect many of the diarrhoeas to respond quickly to that.'

He stayed, working, until the last man had been fully examined, discussing with me quite amicably the border-line cases whose medical disposal was equivocal. It felt like being alongside a well-tried colleague, but I knew the circumstances were exceptional. He was in a good mood, perhaps induced by the festive season, of which I was a gratuitous beneficiary. Tomorrow could be quite different. I was careful to observe the protocol, the accepted formalities of address and approach, careful not to tread on his toes. He could change. The Americans, whose morale had been at a very low ebb, began to recover their spirits as they saw the efforts being made on their behalf. When we had finished, and Brettschneider had departed, I made a final round of the lager. Some, although now warm and relatively comfortable, were still evidently in great mental distress; one or two moaning quietly, calling the names of mother, wife or sweetheart, totally withdrawn, faces turned to the wall.

'Watch those fellows,' I warned the senior soldier, 'their will to recover needs nursing. You know the Krauts who took you prisoner are now being pushed back?'

'Is that so?'

'So we've heard on the BBC. The Ardennes offensive has failed, and your first army has gone over to the attack.'

'Oh boy. That'll cheer them up!'

'Work on them. I'll be in again tomorrow.'

'Thanks a lot Doc. And merry Christmas.'

It had been by no means a merry Christmas so far, but things began to look up when we returned to the revier. Bretiot and two other French doctors were in from Wahren and the corks, or rather the beer bottle tops, were popping. I looked anxiously at Bretiot,

'How are they coping with the new Americans at the hospital?'

'The Yugoslavs are looking after them. It is not their Christmas today,' I looked at him enquiringly, 'the Serbs celebrate it on the twenty-first of January – that will be some party I can tell you.'

'Come on now,' said Denis, 'you have worked hard enough for on day. One ought to begin the celebrations.'

'A moment, if you will forgive me. There is a tradition in British armed forces that at Christmas officers wait on the other ranks. I should visit the ward first. How about it David?'

'They've already had their issue, sir, I didn't know how long you were going to be.'

There had been a special distribution of Red Cross food and diet parcels for the occasion, and David had taken it upon himself to initiate the proceedings in the ward. Still, I felt it incumbent upon me to pay the sick a visit before I did anything else. It was a sense inculcated not only by the army but also by my teaching hospital, where consultants invariably put in an appearance in the wards at midday and, allowing themselves to be rigged out in chef's gear or other fancy-dress, carved the turkey for their patients. So I went round the ward trying to find a word for each man, through no inherent virtue on my part but entirely due to training, and only then did I feel really free to join the 'gang' downstairs and let myself go.

This was my first Christmas as a prisoner; not so the others, for whom it was at least the second, and in one or two cases the fourth. The great theme of this occasion was that it must surely be everybody's last in Germany, and the talk was of where each would be and what he would be doing this time next year. The hilarity increased in direct relation to the number of empties and when, well into the early evening, the Feldwebel appeared bearing half a dozen bottles of wine, and in a very jovial frame of mind, we ran the risk of treating him with overmuch familiarity. He seemed genuinely happy to stay and join our party, but his happiness was bottle-fed. So may ours have been to some extent, but we also had the news from the Ardennes and belief in our near-future liberation as a solid basis for rejoicing, and. I found myself having to bite back the desire to commiserate with him, not to crow, but to tell him how sorry I was that his own future looked so uncertain and dark. But it would not have done. It would be skating on the thin ice of his feelings and it was best to preserve a formal distance. So we exchanged silly jokes and kept the conversation at a superficial level. Eventually he made his uncertain way back downstairs, and Bretiot and his companions were not long in following, leaving us with enough liquid refreshment to see us through until bedtime – a pleasurable mopping-up operation to which we attended with apropriate single-mindedness.

After Christmas there was an abrupt return to the long, long hours of sick-parades and lager visits. Fitting in a daily attendance at the American sub-revier meant cutting into the 'lunch hour'. It never had been an hour, generally no more than thirty or, at the most, forty minutes. Now it was a question of bolting one's food and getting out and about as quickly as possible in the afternoon, returning more often than not somewhere near seven o'clock in the evening. There was now no doubt about the situation in the Ardennes having turned decisively in our favour. The Russians too were advancing. It was all work with, fortunately, undisturbed nights, and time passed unnoticed. Towards the end of the week van Eck announced with considerable satisfaction he had managed to 'acquire' three tickets for a concert to be performed by the internationally famous pianist, Walter Gieseking, at a theatre in Alexandra Platz on Sunday morning, and suggested that he and Denis and I should make use of them. Van Eck was a keen student of classical music, I loved the piano, and Denis saw it is a great opportunity to dress in his best and eye the ladies. It proved to be a very smart, high society occasion for the Leipzigers, the turn-out as chic as anything I had seen in wartime London. Beautiful furs were everywhere in evidence, the theatre being unheated, and I found myself sitting next to one. I stole a glance, expecting to see a feminine owner, and nearly shot out of my seat. It was a Japanese male, with an exceptionally ugly face, who was returning my startled stare with undisguised hostility. I do not know what would have happened next, except I was definitely bent on escaping from the theatre as soon as possible, if the curtain had not at that moment risen, and Gieseking begun his recital, a programme of works by Beethoven. In the interval I turned my back on the Jap and confided my acute anxieties to Denis. He laid a calming hand on my knee.

'Do not distress yourself. He will not do anything. He is probably the guest of some high-ranking official who has lent him the coat to keep him warm.'

'Will you change places?

'Of course. If you wish.'

'I would prefer it.'

After that I was able to relax and enjoy the performance which was superb, closing with a moving rendering of the Moonlight Sonata. It was an absorbing experience that quite shut out the war. I walked dreamily out into the sunshine, entertaining thoughts of the futility of hostilities between nations sharing a common heritage of civilisation, and was at once brutally brought down to earth. On the Platz a Hitler Youth Rally was in noisy, strident process, the boys and girls marching and counter-marching to a martial band, bearing all their tribal emblems, totem poles and other Nazi nonsense past a local führer ensconced on a podium enveloped in swastika, crooked-cross flags.

The contrast was stark; appreciation of beauty within the theatre, wild applause for a great artistic performance, and outside the mindless worship of racial superiority and the cult of the rule of fear. Perhaps it was as well. There was a danger in living so close to the ostensibly pacific daily lives of the Leipzigers; one could begin to identify with them. One needed the reminder of the totally unacceptable Nazi creed to restore the balance.

The first two weeks in January saw a gradual increase in the number of sick and an intensification of the cold, but there were no disturbing air-raids and we simply got on with the work – living each day for itself. Although thoroughly exhausted at the end of it there was nothing to prevent us going to bed as soon as we had had our meal; indeed it was encouraged by the Feldwebel in the interests of saving lighting and heating. I was generally asleep by half-past nine which, with reveille at five-thirty in the morning, afforded me the eight hours I felt I needed.

At about this time a front tooth, broken off almost level with the gum in a very clumsy parachute landing at Arnhem, began to give me rather a lot of pain and I asked, in some trepidation, whether it would be possible to get it seen to. I had never much liked visits to the dentist, and had been hoping I could get by with it until I was liberated. It was no problem. Feldwebel picked up a telephone and made an appointment for me with a Zahnarzt who had a surgery not far from the revier, and I found myself one Saturday afternoon ringing the bell of his door. It was opened by a pleasant looking girl, who introduced herself as his daughter and assistant. He was an elderly but kindly looking man who escorted me to an old fashioned, leather-bound chair, flanked by an equally old-fashioned (by modern standards) treadle-foot drill. I was feeling far from brave yet very conscious of my British uniform. It would not do to flinch. I just hoped he would fix it and, if it had to be painful, very quickly. He hummed to himself as he inspected it, in fact he hummed all through the subsequent proceedings. Perhaps he felt it was soothing for his patients, like the taped music used sometimes today in smart surgeries. He straightened up and regarded me benevolently.

'There is enough tooth left for me to crown it. It would be what I would advise. Better than extracting it. But you can have it out if you prefer.'

'What does the crown entail? How do you do it?'

He rattled off some technicalities but I gathered only the gist of what he was saying, my German being deficient in his field. So I asked him if he would draw it on paper, which he did most artistically. If there was a chance of not having to wear a denture I thought I had better take it, so I braced myself and assented.

Two hours later, my face feeling like a football, and groggy from repeated injections of local anaesthetic, I was on my way back to the revier. He had made a very fine job of my tooth but had made me sweat for it. Not intentionally I am sure. He had to take out the nerve and drill holes for staples. Now and again he touched me on the raw, which kept me on tenterhook everytime he indulged in drilling lest he should hit it again, tensed up and gripping the sides of the chair fit to wrench them from the seat. And all the time I was thinking, I hope to God he knows what he is doing. He was very slow and methodical, and his daughter hovered about solicitously, refilling my glass for the spittoon and smiling encouragingly. They neither of them could have shown more concern to treat me well and fairly, and at the end when I looked at my mouth in his mirror I felt very much in his debt.

'What are the arrangements for payment?' I asked, anxious he should receive his due reward.

'That is not important. I will recover my fee from the government.'

'It has been a pleasure to meet you, and I am most grateful for your services.'

He gave me a straight but hesitant look. 'I would like you to think,' he said, 'that all Germans are not bad Germans, and' he lowered his voice, 'and all Germans are not in favour of the war and,' shaking his head, 'never have been.'

I was taken by surprise at his openness. From Hitler's and the Nazi point of view what he had said was treasonable.

'I am happy to know that,' I said, 'and I deeply appreciate and will respect your confidence.'

On the threshold, as if publicly to implement his private opinion he extended his hand, as did his daughter. I shook them both.

'Auf wiedersehen.'

'Auf wiedersehen.'

On Monday 7 January there was another huge sick parade at the revier, a good two hundred, and among the throng was a man complaining that his head ached, that he felt very tired, and had vague aching pains in his limbs. I could find nothing particularly wrong. His temperature was normal, and there were no physical signs I could elicit to point to a definite diagnosis. If Brettschneider had been at my back I would probably have marked him fit for work, but he wasn't, and some sixth sense, which has to develop in the career of doctoring if bad mistakes are to be avoided, warned me he might be in for something – I knew not what. So I ordered him to bed in his lager, issued him with some aspirins, and told him to come back and see me again on the Friday.

He reappeared, however, on the Wednesday, two days later, scarce able to walk, supported by companions, very out of breath and in obvious distress. I dropped what I was doing and, after putting a stethoscope to his chest had him immediately assisted upstairs and put to bed in the ward. Apart from anything else he had widespread bronchopneumonia. There were a lot of influenzal-type illnesses running through the lagers, La Grippe, Denis called them, and I assumed from the rapidity with which the pneumonia had developed it must be due to a virus. There were no antibiotics available, not that they are effective against virus but they do prevent bacterial superinfection. There was penicillin in Britain and America but none in Germany. The only drug I had to treat this kind of illness was Prontosil, one of the very earliest of the M & B type antibacterials that had in fact originated in Germany.

He by now had a high temperature, increasing difficulty in breathing, and by the evening I became very concerned. I got Denis to see him with me and we were agreed he was in urgent need of oxygen. Meanwhile, Denis suggested we resorted to 'cupping'. It was not something I had ever seen used at my medical school. Denis said it would do no harm and might make the patient feel more comfortable. He sent for Maire, the expert, and in no time, having warmed their interiors with a taper, he had rows of small glass jars adhering to the patient's back and raising round red marks.

Then began an infuriating battle with German red-tape. The Feldwebel raised Brettschneider on the phone for me and I told him the situation, asking if oxygen could be delivered urgently to the revier.

'Nein. Patients needing oxygen must be transferred to the hospital.'

'He needs it right away.'

'Nein. It is the rule. Patients needing oxygen must be transferred to the hospital.'

This was a different Brettschneider from the one who had helped me with the Americans. I argued with him to no avail. He was adamant. It was the rule.

'How long will it be before an ambulance can get here?'

'I do not know. If they are not in use it will not be long.'

'The ambulance will bring some oxygen?'

'Nein. Oxygen stays in the hospital. It is the rule.'

'But this patient is very ill.'

'He will recover when he gets to hospital. That is the end of it,' I heard the click the other end as he put the phone down.

Stubborn bastard. I turned to the Feldwebel who was looking sympathetic 'Tell me as soon as the ambulance gets here. I shall be up in the ward.'

David was sitting anxiously by the bed, supporting the poor fellow as he strove to cough up the secretions accumulating in his lungs. It was a harrowing experience for everyone in the room. As for myself, I was in a rage, not only with Brettschneider but with my own helplessness. Nothing is more infuriating to a medical man than to see a disease progressing in the wrong direction despite all his efforts. When he doesn't know the cause or what to do it is worse. Sometimes this ignorance can engender such a sense of guilt he takes it out on the object of its arousal, the poor patient, by giving short shrift or scant attention. But ignorance, here and there, unless culpable through failure to self-educate, is one of the inevitable terms of reference of medical practice. We have to live with it. As it happened I was not ignorant about this patient's condition, only frustrated that I could do no more to help him.

In due course he was taken to the hospital at Wahren where, despite every care from the Yugoslavian physician-in-charge in person, he died, some thirty-six hours later.

About a week had passed after this sad incident when a man visited me from his lager who said he hoped I would not mind, but he thought he ought to tell me there was considerable feeling in the camp against me because of the death. A vociferous section were saying I did not care a damn whether a man died or not, that I made careless and inadequate examinatians during sick-parade, that I was hand-in-glove with the Germans, and much wild talk of a similar nature. In my informer's opinion it would be politic on my part to write to the camp leader explaining the circumstances, or else they might, he felt, make real trouble for me. I could not quite fathom my informer's motive in telling me this, nor what he might be implying by 'trouble' – a lynching perhaps at my next visit? Naturally I felt very upset, and did sit down and compose a letter to the camp leader setting forth the facts. But I never sent it. I have it before me now. It is headed,

To <u>Camp Leader</u>
Lager 225.   17/1/45
and begins,
'It has come to my notice ...'

On reflection I could well understand their reported feelings, but I knew I had nothing, in this case, for which to reproach myself. Let them complain and I would explain next time I visited. They would have ample opportunity as I visited their camp, on average, three times a week. I was glad I did not send the letter for I heard nothing more about it, and encountered no overt hostility whatsoever.

The rest of the week was dominated by news of Russian advances on all fronts. On the day I wrote the letter they were reported this side of Warsaw and making steady progress westwards. When, on Sunday 21st,

I attended Wahren hospital for the Serbian Christmas celebrations, the atmosphere was muted by the growing, almost tangible apprehension concerning the near future, and what it might hold for Leipzig. The day turned out to be the high-water mark of any 'fun' we had been able to extract from our circumstances. We drank our fill for the last time. From then on the days grew grimmer and grimmer.

To begin with there was a resumption of large-scale air-raids. Russians, Zhukov's army, reached the river Oder at a point a mere 100 miles east of Leipzig on 1 February, and the raids pointed to a softening-up process preliminary to the next, probably decisive push from east and west. Every morning, at about noon the siren went off, wailing exactly as in England. The Americans were over the Reich in strength. The Feldwebel now insisted, as soon as the alarm sounded, that all prisoners descended to the cellars. If I was in the middle of a sick-parade the whole business was interrupted for two or more hours, the Americans playing merry hell with whatever target they had chosen in our zone, while we loitered below wondering and waiting, far too crowded together to continue with any medical work. I felt schizophrenic. Part of me was not unpleased the Germans were receiving a daylight pasting, proof of Allied power – anything if it would shorten the war, but another part of me hoped fervently it would not be Leipzig that caught it. The raids moreover made my job that much more difficult, and I could not dissociate myself from the adverse effects they were having on my daily life. Publicly we all put up a bold front, telling the Feldwebel and other German staff in the revier they should stop fighting unless they wanted to see Leipzig destroyed. No amount of hiding in cellars could save anyone, as we had bombs able to penetrate double the depth. We affected a nonchalant and devil-may-care attitude craning our heads out of the window and waving whenever we thought we heard an Allied machine passing over, which happened not infrequently without a warning, to the eternal annoyance of the Germans who, for some reason, believed that any prisoner pointing or waving was signalling for a bomb to be dropped on himself.

I put in a formal complaint to the Feldwebel at being made to interrupt my work and go down to the cellar every time the siren went. I told him I considered it an insult. I had been through much of the German bombing of London, and knew when it was time to take cover without being told. But he would not give way.

'You are all my responsibility,' he said sadly, 'if anything happens to you I will be blamed. I cannot take the risk.'

So we were in the ironic position of being forcibly protected by the enemy against the risk of being killed by our own side.

The daylight raids were followed up by regular incursions of the RAF at night. They put in an appearence at about 9 pm. The German Radio announcer would say, 'Leipzig transmitter now closing down as enemy aircraft are approaching. We wish you pleasant listening elsewhere and hope to be back with you soon.' Then we would pack our bags and wait for the siren which, being situated on some gas works the other side of York Platz, always sounded very loud and made me jump. Once the siren had gone there was nothing for it but another weary descent to the cellar, helping the patients down and bedding them on the mattresses with which it was furnished. I sometimes caught glimpses of the Russian doctor and his orderlies, whose quarters were in the lower part of the building, but all the time I was in Leipzig I never achieved a meeting with him. Denis had made his acquaintance and reported him to be a decent enough fellow, not too happy at the prospect of being liberated by his own side. The Russians recognised neither the Red Cross nor the status of prisoner of war in respect of their own nationals. According to our information Russians were ordered not to surrender. Prisoners therefore were officially non-existent.

An immediate side-effect of the new air offensive was to cause an ever-increasing scarcity of food. Apart from factories manufacturing war materials, raids, the BBC insisted, were aimed at communications, railway martialling yards in particular. The trickle of Red Cross food parcels dried up completely and the German army ration, to which we were reduced, itself suffered from supply problems. Soup became the staple, soup for every meal with a slice or two of black bread, and sausage if we were lucky. It was monotonous and low in nutriment and it began to affect the resistance of the prisoners to illness with an accompanying increase in the numbers going sick. I myself developed a bad cold, complicated by an infection in the sinuses. There was nothing to do for it but take aspirins, carry on and try to forget about it, but I could feel myself flagging mentally and physically.

There had been raids in the vicinity, and on some of the outskirts of Leipzig, but none near POW areas or on the main part of the city. February rains had set in, the snow had melted and travelling around was consequently that much easier – something on the bonus side. On the other hand I had serious outbreaks of streptococcal tonsillitis in some of the lagers, and in one of them I was horrified to find a case of diphtheria. I pressed the Brettschneider panic button and he came racing onto the scene in a battered old Mercedes, agreed my diagnosis, and drove the man in his own car to the hospital for isolation and treatment. I took the closest contacts to the revier and isolated them in a corner of the ward where I could keep a close watch on them. The occupants of the lager were all taken off work and confined to their building. One of the men in the revier went down with it but that was all. I considered we had been lucky.

At the hospital I had the opportunity of talking to some American airmen who had baled out of a stricken Flying Fortress. I had already had some old-standing prisoner aviators in the revier who had been dropped off for treatment from columns being forced away from prison camps threatened by the Russians. All without exception had been most eager to be on their way, and out of the city, which they thought was a dangerous place to be in. I was struck therefore by the indifference of the Americans to the threat of raids by their own colleagues.

'No need to worry buddy. The whereabouts of this and the other POW hospital, your revier and most of the lagers is known to our people. They'll be avoided if humanly possible.'

If humanly possible. Some comfort at least.

On 7 February we learned that the Ardennes salient had been completely reduced and operations had begun to clear the way for a crossing of the Rhine. We estimated the Americans were now about 200 hundred miles to the west of us; double the distance of the Russians who, nevertheless, were still halted on the far side of the Oder. The Germans in the revier now started to exhibit a marked indifference to the outcome of the war. The Feldwebel was quite open in expressing his opinion the sooner it was over the better and, air-raids apart, became less and less concerned about enforcing the rules laid down for the control of prisoners. The Gestapo, on the other hand, stepped up their activity and started to pay us regular visits, keeping, I supposed, a finger on points of possible insurrection. The Feldwebel, well aware that we possessed maps, a camera and a radio, and content to wink at these forbidden fruits as long as we kept him up to date with our news bulletins, having got wind of the Gestapo visits, now hastily tipped us off, collected these items and secured them in a locker in his office. Thereafter he listened to the BBC with us but kept the radio locked in his room. If the Gestapo had rumbled him he would have been for it. He had staked himself out on our side. These unsmiling, sinister, hard-faced men visited in pairs, sporting long black mackintoshes and felt hats, exactly as reputed, and rummaged around the building escorted by the Feldwebel, while we carried on with whatever we were doing and affected not to notice tham. It was always a relief when they had gone, above all to the Feldwebel. After one visit he was so pleased to see the back of them he beceme quite euphoric,

'It is a fine day, why do you not go out and find yourself a nice Fraulein?'

'A Fraulein' I stuttered, 'you cannot be serious.'

'Why not?' he replied, leering at me, 'A man is a man. Nothing matters any more.'

I had not been able properly to throw off my sinusitis, and a week later went down with a *bona fide* dose of influeza, the real thing; high temperature, severe headache, pains in the body and limbs, a crawling skin and total prostration. I became Denis' patient. He put me to bed, fed me aspirin and prontosil, and arranged for one of his colleagues from the POW hospital to take on my sick-parades and visits. I stayed in bed several days, fortunately during a lull in air-raids. It was bad having nothing obligatory to occupy my mind. The 'flu' brought with it a lassitude that took away any desire to work at my German, or medical textbooks. I listened to the German radio, read their newspapers, and feverishly compared them with the bulletins David brought me from the BBC. I became haunted by conviction that unless the Germans very soon capitulated I should not live to see England again – no-one would. A doom-laden sense of the Arnhem-like holocaust that might rage in Leipzig if the Germans fought to hold it street by street obsessed my mind. I could think of nothing else by day, and dreamed of nothing else by night. I now realise my mental state was a product of the 'flu', the well-recognised post-influenzal depression, but then I was too desolated to have insight into my own condition. Finding it intolerable I transferred the hatefulness of it to all Germans in general and to Brettschneider in particular. The fact he continued to support the war, and to lord it over me, combined to foster such a strong feeling of resentment against him I found myself phantasising scenes, as I lay in bed, in which I let him have it, where our roles were reversed, where *he* was beholden to *me*, obliged to tread warily and speak *my* language.

Once I had recovered sufficiently to get about and start work again I quickly became too busy for any conscious thoughts to fester further along those lines, but I was still weak and found the effort of coping with the day's stint very exhausting. I knew I was short-tempered and irritable, and occasionally was aware of Denis looking at me with some concern. But I did not know exactly how fragile the catch on the lid of my self-control had become.

On the last Wednesday in February, the 22nd, I rose at my usual hour preparatory to starting the big sick-parade at seven o'clock. A day or two previously I had received some very welcome news. The POW hospital at Wahren had been reinforced by a British doctor taken at Arnhem, Major Brian Courtney of the 133 Parachute Field Ambulance, whose commanding officer had been Bill Alford. British prisoners in the hospital had always to some extent been disadvantaged by the language barrier existing between themselves and the medical staff. The doctors did their very best, that I knew, but the prisoners could not always get across to them the exact nature of their complaints, and I was at times convinced inappropriate treatments were instituted based on misdiagnoses. This left me with the difficult diplomatic task of suggesting to the Serbs, Italians or French that another regime might be preferable to the one recommended, a task made more difficult still by my relative youth and short POW experience The establishing of a resident British doctor not only meant our nationals would be under the direct care of one of themselves, but I would be relieved of the necessity to visit them, at least every Sunday, sometimes more often, to see how they were getting on. I couldn't wait to make contact with Courtney.

Denis and I took up our usual positions at the end of the room in front of the table, the queues began their slow shuffle towards us and we were soon going flat out. At ten o'clock Brettschneider arrived. I was already feeling very fatigued and threw him but a brief nod of recognition as he went to the table behind me. I could hear him riffling through the notes I had made on the patients already seen, and knowing he would very soon start to ask me questions and feeling in need of a respite, I unthinkingly perched myself on the edge of the table with my back to him. Then, with Courtney on my mind, I, again unthinkingly, opened a conversation, throwing my words over my shoulder.

'They tell me I have a British colleague at the hospital. When did he arrive?'

There was an ominous silence, at least I know now it was ominous, followed by a barked order from Brettschneider,

'Stand up and turn round.'

I was slow to comply, my warning antennae blunted by my labours.

'Schnell. Schnell.'

At that I did slip off the table and make a casual about turn.

Brettschneider's eyes were blazing and his hands, knuckles resting on the table, tightly clenched.

'Such a display of bad manners from any prisoner,' he spat out the word, 'I have never seen, let alone from a so-called gentleman.'

I felt hot blood rising up from my neck and opened my mouth, not to say anything, but from sheer surprise.

'Silence. I have not finished.'

'But ...'

'Silence. Have you not learnt yet that you stand to attention when a German officer enters the room? Should you not have done so when I entered? And should you not at least have said, "good morning Herr Stabsarzt"? And should you not, if you wished to address me, have had the courtesy to look at me? Eh? eh?'

I opened and closed my mouth like a fish in a tank.

'Perhaps I should send you to a German school to learn how a gentle-man,' he said it with sneering emphasis, 'should behave.'

By now I realised I had undoubtedly been careless with this protocol-insistent overlord. But the knowledge was an added irritant. Suddenly I found myself thinking, dammit I'm on the winning side, an he's on the losing. He is lost, done for. He's had it. Why the hell should I put up with his bloody orders any longer. And the lid came off – right off.

'Captain.' I said in English, deliberately placing my hands on the table in exact imitation of his own, and leaning towards him, 'I am not obliged under the Geneva Convention to do any of the things you said, nor to listen to your insults.'

It was the turn of his mouth to drop open. He looked at me in utter disbelief. 'Deutsche sprecken. Deutsche. Verstehen Sie? Und aufstehen.'

His voice had gone up several semitones and decibels, but his indigna-tion only sparked off a greater desire to achieve his humiliation.

'I will not speak German. I will not stand up. And you can go to hell.'

Van Eck was wringing his hands, the Feldwebel flashing me stern glances, Denis watching warily, and the whole room had gone deadly silent.

I was now beside myself, reckless of consequences, all the angry feel-ings repressed during my captivity fuelling my aggression. The words rushed out.

'And let me tell you, captain, in a few weeks' time you will be the prisoner. You would do well to think of that. My report on you will be called for, and acted upon.'

Brettschneider held his position, glowering. Without taking his eyes off me he called to van Eck. 'Translate into German please.'

Van Eck looked at me appealingly.

'Tell him. Tell him. Word for word.'

Van Eck began to prevaricate.

'Tell him.' I snapped, still leaning toward Brettschneider, both of us breathing hard.

As van Eck hesitantly but accurately relayed my words, Brettschneider's face, hitherto flushed, went very pale. I was watching him closely and thought to myself, that's got him, he's frightened now. I was experienc-ing something akin to exultation, reliving my sick-bed phantasies in a way the opportunity for which seldom comes. But my phantasies, like all phantasies, were deceivers.

Brettschneider took his hands off the table, stood up straight and with great deliberation, withdrew the pistol he always carried from its holster and pointed it straight at my chest.

'Aufstehen, stabsarzt.'

I went further off the rails. 'Don't you dare point that bloody thing at me,' I shouted, lunging across with the wild intention of knocking it out of his hand.

Brettschneider merely stepped back a pace, motioning me upwards with the point of his pistol.

'Aufstehen' he shouted back.

It was then I felt restraining hands, Denis gently but firmly prising me from my position at the table, and edging himself between myself and Brettschneider, and heard David saying urgently into my ear,

'He's capable of pulling the trigger. Do what he says, sir, for God's sake, and don't say any more.'

I stood, more or less at attention, van Eck on one side, David on the other, each holding an arm, while Denis in his faultless German spoke soothingly to Brettschneider.

'Please Herr Stabsarzt. Le médecin capitaine is not well. He is very nervous. Not fully recovered from severe Grippe. Very tired and overworked. You know how it can be. He does not realise what he is saying. After he has rested he will send you an apology. I will see to it. I will guarantee it.'

Whether it was Denis' words or the fact I was now standing as he had ordered, albeit by the restraint placed on me by van Eck and David, Brettschneider slowly lowered his pistol and put it back in its holster. Denis went on talking, repeating variations on what he had already said. He was right. I didn't like to admit it but I was very tired. Quite suddenly I felt all the stuffing go out of me. The reaction had set in. I became conscious of all the sick still waiting to be seen, of all the daunting work that lay ahead. It was time to capitulate.

'Entschuldigen Sie bitte, Herr Stabsarzt. Darf Ich noch einmal arbeiten?'

He eyed me balefully for a few moments, then nodded his head and motioned me towards the patients.

'Bitte.'

Somehow or other I got through the rest of the morning, but after I had finished the work I found I had no appetite for food and fell wearily onto my bed. Denis followed me into the room.

'Thank you,' I said to him, 'You are a good friend. You probably saved my life.'

'Everything you did and said was very understanderable. You remember Jean at Naunhof?'

'Of course.'

'He had a pistol pulled on him in his early days here. But as for me, I am too old to rage at them. It is futile, useless. I prefer the diplomatic game. It will not be for long. Germans like Brettschneider will keep up their façade until the end. Then they will disappear. You will see. They will make their way back to their home, bury their uniforms and start again, as if nothing had ever happened.

'And now?'

'Now we go along with them. Truly it is the best way.' He brightened 'You know, it is my birthday the day after tomorrow?' I shook my head 'No? I shall be thirty. Let us forget all about this morning and think about having a party. I have a feeling Brettschneider will be leaving us alone for a period. He will not want to risk another encounter like that with you. It is bad for his dignity.'

'If I hurt that it is something. Tell me, do you really see me as being neuveux?'

'The word does not mean quite the same in French as it does in English. It connotes excitability rather than timidity. Bien sur. You have had to work harder than any of us because you have been the only Britisher. You have been under a strain and the Grippe has finished you off. You exhibit all the symptoms of nervous exhaustion.'

Do I now, I thought. So that's how I look to others. I suppose every doctor likes to think he is perfectly capable of knowing his own health, mental as well as physical. It was chastening to see myself through Denis' eyes. He obviously thought I had flipped my top. Perhaps I had. 'And now?' I had asked him. Now I must make a fresh start, husband my inner resources for the last lap; to regain the light of day. That must be the task.

In Leipzig, as in London, citizens' morale was apparently understood as something in those days that depended, to some extent, on maintaining an adequate supply of beer, at least, in pubs and clubs. Nobody took much interest in food for its own sake, it was far too monotonous and dull. But alcohol to anaesthetise fears, release tensions and promote jollity was something that mattered in those grim times and we in the revier still had cigarettes. I had never been a serious smoker and found no great difficulty in giving up in favour of hoarding, when it opened the doors to so much power of purchase. So, for Denis' part there was beer to be bought, the means to buy it, and we had a skinful. Inside the mess we stuck a notice on the door.

38

mais

120

A joke. In French the figures read: trente-huit mais cent-vigt, and cent vingt sounds as well like sans vin – without wine. We thought it hilariously funny. Every time we filled our mugs – we drank everything from mugs – we toasted the notice, and ended up sprawling in the chairs, telling stories and singing doubtful songs; not exactly the popular image of responsible doctors, but appropriate to the occasion. There had not been much to smile about in recent weeks and a good uninhibited hair-down guffaw was long overdue. I began the next day with the inevitable hangover, but also with a much-improved sense of proportion. To survive was the priority. I would direct my words and behaviour entirely to that end, use my head, keep cool. There must be no more foolish outbursts.

Survival however, on Monday 27 February, became something that hung by the thread, not of how I conducted myself but, of the inscrutable workings of providence. The usual, therefore not unexceptional afternoon siren went off on the gasworks at 2 o'clock, and we all descended to the cellar. I had been involved in another interminable sick-parade and only just then finished. Grabbing a couple of pieces of bread and slapping some slices of sausage between them, I went to supervise the movement of the patients, then followed with my own gear and took up a standing position under an arched entrance to one of the chambers, from where I could observe the British patients occupying it, and the Feldwebel and his staff, who held a position in a recess near the foot of the stairs. A lot of prisoners were obliged to stand as the revier had recently been augmented by sick men dropped off from forced marches, the installation of additional bunks, and the atmosphere in the cellar soon became very stale.

I munched my sandwiches irritably. It really was the limit, this waste of valuable time. After three-quarters of an hour of waiting I became overcome with impatience and moved over to the Feldwebel who was listening to the German air-raid bulletin on his radio.

'How much longer have we to stay down here Feldwebel?' I asked him. 'Surely it must all be over now?'

He shook his head. 'There is a very large bomber force coming this way. But they may be going to Halle.'

I shrugged my shoulders and sauntered back to my previous post. The men were quietly chatting and joking. I told them the score, and offered a few desultory remarks on any old topic that suggested itself, never taking my eyes off the Feldwebel for very long. Oh come on. Surely. Another ten minutes passed. Then he and the guards suddenly jumped up and hastily started to cram on their steel helmets. We knew what this meant. They always did it when the wireless announced raiders as being in the immediate vicinity and expected to fly over the city.

Soon, unmistakably, came the drone of approaching aircraft, and everyone stopped talking and listened. The Feldwebel went to the top of the stairs and opened the door. It might have been a sign for at once we heard explosions, and he slammed the door and hurried back down the stairs, announcing, quite unnecessarily,

'They are here.'

Almost immediately the cellar began to vibrate. The noise of multiple engines rose in a crescendo, from a growl to a menacing roar, and the bombs began to fall in earnest; an unbelievable avalanche of explosives, stunning the senses. The bombs had no separate identity, with individual whistles and crashes such as I had become accustomed to in London. There were so many the effect was of an endless procession of express trains all tearing out of the sky towards the same spot; and I was on it hopelessly and helplessly tied. The ground beneath us trembled and heaved. The overall noise became shattering, horrific, an orchestrated nightmare of snarling low-flying aircraft, screaming bomb-falls and thunderous explosions. The end of the world, our world, had surely arrived. I watched the ceiling and walls shimmering as in a heat haze, the atmosphere thickening with cascades of mortar dust. Then, suddenly, the lights went out and we were plunged into darkness. I was grateful. It hid my fear. I had put on what I hoped was a reassuring smile for the benefit of the patients when it started. Now I could feel the corners of my mouth draw back, baring my clenched teeth, in uncontrolled spasm, as in the *risus sardonicus* of tetanus. I believed myself to be on the very threshold of death, the building about to fall and bury us all at any moment. A catchphrase from medical student days came into my head 'the feeling of impending dissolution'. This was it. I had known it before, at Arnhem. The same. As if the pit of the stomach were an expanding void, with two giant fists driving inexorably, one upward the other downward, compressing, compressing, making it harder and harder to breathe, heart and lungs choking up the throat; harder and harder to hold back an evacuation from viscera at bursting point in the pelvis.

But at Arnhem the consoling thought had at one time come to me, if this is what it is like to be on the verge of death it is not totally insupportable. I grabbed hold of that again. There cannot be anything harder to come. I could not possibly feel any worse. The next must be black-out. Another voice came, unbidden, 'you can stand it. You can stand it, literally'. So compelling was it that, if I had not already been on my feet, I would have risen. Who said I can stand it? It puzzled me. Had I heard it said somehere before? My mind became occupied with the question, distracted by it, until at last I got it. The echo from a past lesson. St Paul. 'Take unto you the whole armour of God that ye may be able to withstand in the evil day, and having done all to stand. Stand therefore ...' Endlessly I repeated these words, trying to remember what came after 'therefore' – the details of the armour of God. But they escaped me, beneficially; for in the mental exercise of the pursuit I was led away from total preoccupation with my fear, and the pressures receded. My breathing eased. I did not evacuate.

Eventually, as from a dream, I awoke to the fact the noise had stopped, the Germans had lit candles and Feldwebel, distantly, from somewhere beyond the top of the stairs was shouting something about 'fire'. His shout seemed to strike off the chains of paralysis that had bound my limbs and I bounded up to join him where he now stood, a red spotted handerkerchief covering his nose and mouth. The front door had been blown open, smoke was billowing in from the street, and he was on the threshold surveying the scene outside.

'Is it finished now?' I panted.

'Not officially.' Not officially. Dear old Feldwebel. I felt like embracing him. 'But,' he pointed, 'I want volunteers to help pull furniture out of there.'

Separated from us only by the ruins of the house adjacent destroyed in a raid before my time, were four in the same row blazing furiously. I glanced up at the revier. All the windows smashed but no smoke coming out anywhere. It was black as night, save for the lurid glare of flames, everything enveloped in smoke clouds. The road was littered with debris and a rain of ash was still falling, dirtying our uniforms.

'Are there any people in those burning houses?' I asked breathlessly

'No. They will all have gone to the main shelter. But we may be able to save some of their things from the downstairs rooms.'

I returned to the cellar and told the men the position. Activity for the able-bodied, was the best sort of medicine after such an experience as we had all been through. But I gave them to understand the raid might not yet be over, and they were under no obligation to risk their lives for bits of enemy furniture.

While a volunteer squad under the Feldwebel set about their task of salvage, Denis and I collected a few things from the treatment room and went out, further afield, to see if there was anyone in the vicinity in need of medical assistance. It was now uncannily quiet, only the crackle of flames breaking the silence, until suddenly the all-clear sounded from the York siren. The gas works had, unbelievably, survived. Soon the streets became full of poeple rushing about and shouting. Several shook their fists at us. But we were known as doctors in the neighbour-hood, were wearing our Red Cross armbands and there were no nasty incidents. Not so in other parts of the city where, I heard later, British prisoners had been stoned by the vengeful populace.

139

We came upon a large bomb crater not more than twenty-five yards from our front door. We had been amazingly fortunate. The raid had lasted an inteminable forty minutes and we had been spared high explosives and incendiaries. A reconnaissance later showed that a section of Leipzig, among others, starting a mere hundred yards from the revier had been completely taken out, totally flattened. The devastation in this area had also stopped short of the POW hospital situated in the northern part of the city, but the main thoroughfares linking them with the revier were unrecognisable and impassable. ARP services were totally disorganised and all public transport at a standstill. Luckily there was little or no risk of the fires nearby spreading to the revier as we were separated by the ruin, but there was no way of putting them out and they blazed furiously all the rest of the day and during the night, sending up pillars of flame as roof and floors collapsed and dropped into the inferno.

Water, electricity and gas were all interrupted, the Feldwebel having in any case turned off the latter at the supply point as part of his routine air-raid precautions, and now many mains were fractured even if the gasometer was still in one piece. We were unable to cook or wash, and drinking water had to be fetched from standpipes happily found still in operation some distance from the revier. With all the windows blown out it became very cold inside, and murky from the in-drifting smoke. Work among the patients was carried on by the light of flickering candles. They lay fully clothed under their blankets, we bundled up in sweaters and overcoats.

The evening bulletin from the BBC was full of the news of our visitation. 'Two thousand Flying Fortresses today attacked railway communications and war factories in the city of Leipzig in Saxony. Very little opposition was encountered from the enemy and the raid was a complete success'. The strike was seen to be of strategic value in reducing the potential of Leipzig as a serious obstacle to the renewed advance of the Allied armies, from whichever direction it might come, east or west. We could not help but see it also as a strike against civilian morale and the will to continue the war. Casualties were astronomical. Broad swathes of the city ceased to exist. If we had not, fortuitously, been on the very edge of one of them we could not possibly have survived. We had known about the similar raid on Dresden and felt its effects, in a serious reduction in medical supplies, but had somehow failed to see it as a warning of what might happen to Leipzig. Leipzig had already received considerable attention and perhaps we thought, wishfully, it was now low on the priority list of targets. But with Dresden back in mind the awful prospect opened up of the possibility of the RAF, as in that case, following up the daylight raid with one of their own tonight – of even greater intensity using the fires as beacons to mark their targets. From the upper windows of the revier numerous blazes were visible, and it was van Eck who first voiced the dire thought, 'I fear they will be back.' But he was not the only one. The Feldwebel made a point of asking me if I thought the RAF would come and I, out of devilment or bravado, said, 'almost certainly, and it is a pity we have these fires next door.' He saw the point very quickly, and I had the perverse satisfaction of seeing him convey my words to his staff and anxious looks appearing on their faces as the result. One of them came up to me casually, as though he was not really interested, and asked me what I thought about the RAF ten-ton bombs, which had received wide publicity in the German press. I cheerfully told him that if they were dropped on Leipzig it would cease to exist, no-one would escape destruction, and added that the possibility of this happening increased every day that they, the Germans, went on fighting the war which they could not possibly win. 'It is terrible,' he said, 'but what can we possibly do?'

The point I had made to the Germans was now sticking in to myself. I began to prickle with apprehension, and found it very difficult to be reassuring with the patients when they asked me, during my last evening round, what I thought might happen next. They had no illusions, they feared the worst; after all it was the most logical thing to expect. But they still managed to joke it off. 'No need to worry,' said one, 'the Brylcreem boys'll be too busy looking at themselves in the mirror to find their way here.' 'I've a brother in the RAF,' said another, 'if 'e comes near 'ere I won't arf tear 'im orf a strip, an' if 'e kills me I'll wring 'is bleedin' neck'. Thus the humour of even the sick British soldier prevails over circumstances and, I believe, wins wars.

Anxiously we watched the clock and listened to the German radio for any sign of a big attack. Denis had a thought.

'Why do we not go down to the cellar now, anyway? It will be much warmer down there.'

'I was hoping I would never have to see it again.'

'Better to wait. They may not come.'

We sat on, or rather lay on our beds, fully dressed, while the minutes passed, then the hours, and at midnight, as nothing had happened, we went properly to bed, feeling that even if we had to get up again half-an-hour later it would be better than being cold. The next thing I knew it was morning, and the Feldwebel was rousing us at our usual hour. The night had passed without the threatened event. I felt like a condemned man reprieved from the gallows. If they had not come during this night, Denis and I reasoned, when the opportunity for stoking the fires was at its best, then it is more than probable they consider they have given

Leipzig enough to think about for a while. And so it proved.

The immediate days ahead were beset with difficulties, and we lived from hand to mouth. Sewage was a problem owing to the interruption of the water supply, but the drains were usable and the able-bodied among us were obliged to spend many hours a day fetching containers of water, jerry-cans, in from the stand pipes to fill the lavatory cisterns, and the chains were not pulled until at least three persons had used the facilities. The disruption was such that formal visits to and from the lagers was impossible. Trams were not yet running. Deserving sick were brought to see me in the revier by circuitous detours in commandeered vehicles. Others were similarly transported to the hospitals. For the best part of a week we were isolated in the revier. Telephone connections were the first to be restored but the Feldwebel was communicating directly with the Chefarzt, at Oschatz. Brettschneider was conspicuous by his absence. Had he been killed? I did not like to ask the Feldwebel, who had his hands full. In any case none of us had a real interest in the welfare of Brettschneider. We just wondered where he was.

By dint of the most tremendous exertions on the part of the populace, and by putting every available prisoner to work, the Germans determinedly won back order out of the chaos. After a raid on such an oppressive scale the feeling of relief of the survivors at still being in one piece releases a great wave of pent up energy directed at picking up the pieces and starting again. I know this was how it affected me and, to judge by their activity, the Germans. Communications were the number one priority. Streets were steadily cleared and reopened, or abandoned as being beyond reclaim. Tramlines were relaid or rerouted, electricity restored. Supplies began to trickle through to where the need was greatest, water pipes were mended, and gas last of all the services. After that came the demolition of unstable shells of buldings and the sad recovery of corpses. I saw it all. No raid of theirs, not even on Coventry, had been on such a scale. The London blitz, of which I had some experience, having been on the roof of St Thomas's Hospital as a student, fire watching, was harrowing enough but more drawn out, the damage more scattered. Leipzig, in parts had been turned into a desolate wilderness, no longer recognisable, landmarks obliterated, a blackened desert of rubble and fallen masonry.

Denis and I did simply what the day demanded. We spoke not at all of the future. We did not know if there was one. Then, exactly one week after the raid, the Feldwebel called me into his office. He had just received orders from the Chefarzt; I was to return immediately to Naunhof, and take up duty again as Resident British Medical Officer in the revier.

I could scarcely believe my ears and yet, curiously, I felt no elation. Circumstances had forged a bond between Denis, the others, and myself,

cemented stronger by the hardships recently shared, and I was actually loth to leave. The Feldwebel, as usual when it came to moves, had
no explanation. I wondered if I was being posted at the instigation of
Brettschneider, but Denis thought there was more likely to be a general
reshuffle taking place, with the changed pattern of work in Leipzig and
the movement of so many prisoners from the active war zones.

'I do not think we shall meet again until the war is over,' he said as we
shook hands, 'I hope you will come and visit me in France.'

'And I hope you will come and visit me in England.' Banal words to
cover an emotional parting. As I came to say good-bye to van Eck, David,
le Maire, Petit and the patients, I felt as if I were abandoning a sinking
ship, and found myself choking with apologies for going. With the
Feldwebel it was, if anything, worse. On an impulse I snatched a piece of
paper off his desk and wrote;

Revier
Gneisenau Strasse
Leipzig
6 Mar 45

To Whom it may Concern
I wish to testify that the bearer of this certificate has at all times conducted himself towards me and my fellow prisoners with the utmost
consideration for our welfare, and with the utmost correctness in
accordance with the requirements of the Geneva Convention.
I wish to commend him very favourably to whomsoever he may
become subject in the Allied Forces

Signed. Stuart Mawson. Captain, RAMC.

'Take this,' I said, 'Keep it safe. It may be of some help to you. Good
luck. Auf wiedersehen.'

He drew himself into a position of attention, and as I had my beret on,
dressed for the journey, I saluted him.

VII

Naunhof
(6 March – 21 April 1945)

Leipzig station had not, for reasons best known to planners of the raid, suffered a great deal of damage, and trains were moving in and out on regular, if restricted, schedules by the time I left the city – at least in the direction of Naunhof. As I sat by the window of my compartment and watched suburbs giving way to country I experienced a great lifting of spirits and renewal of hope. As Leipzig receded in real distance so it did in thought until, by the time I reached Naunhof I felt as though every connection with that phase of my life had been severed and I had become entirely reorientated to the future.

Approaching the revier I looked at it with affection, quickening my step as if anxious to be home again. Nothing seemed to have changed. It was as if I was just coming in again from a walk, as if I had never really been away. Jean, Alex and Larry seemed genuinely pleased to see me, even the old Obergefreite's face creased into a smile of welcome. I just picked up the threads where I had left them, starting naturally enough with an exchange of news.

Webster had been moved, whether to make way for me or for other reasons no-one knew. Jean said they had watched the raid, just visible and audible from the upper rooms; the Fortresses had indeed been an awe-inspiring sight flying in relatively low, but not feeling themselves to be in any danger they had found the whole thing very exhilarating as evidence of Allied might and power. Indeed the whole atmosphere in the revier was of cheerful optimism and confidence in an early end to the war. In Leipzig we had been so preoccupied with our immediate predicament we had lost track of events. The Western Allies had broken the defences of the Siegfried Line and were now poised, ready for a crossing, along the whole length of the Rhine, from Monty in the north at Nijmegen to the American 7th Army in the south at Strasbourg. There was a feeling in the air of imminent liberation. Everybody had his tail up. Supplies of Red Cross parcels had been down to a trickle at Christmas and then ceased but there was no real shortage of edibles. The bakery next door was working unabated and the French were still working in food shops. The first meal I had was a delicious *choux farci* – scooped out cabbage stuffed and baked with mincemeat and onions – with fresh black bread, washed down with a glass of good milk. The country people knew how to look after themselves. I could not believe my luck, yet I knew over-rejoicing was premature. The strategic analyses emanating from the discussions we had had in Leipzig were not to be lightly dismissed. Life was likely to become uncertain and dangerous, even here, as the corridor narrowed between Russians and Americans. Leipzig had matured me, if maturity is seeing things as they really are and not as one would wish them to be. I found myself taking up a position of leadership, dissuading Jean and the others from counting their chickens and prompting them to join me in preparing contingency plans for the options that might be open to us as events developed.

The very next day the news came through that the 1st American Army had captured, intact, a bridge over the Rhine at Remagen, some twenty miles south of Bonn, and unexpectedly, like a forerunner, an American captain who had lost an eye came to be billetted on the revier. Jean and I fixed him up in our room and he soon became very much one of us. Being used to a huge workload time could very well have hung heavy on my hands, but he played a good game of cribbage and we passed many a long hour with a well-thumbed pack of cards. He and I were entirely of one mind on the need to prepare seriously for the final dénouement, and it seemed to us it might come in one of three different ways.

There might be a formal armistice with the present Nazi govenment still in control, in which case everything should be fairly orderly. There might be a break-up from within with a coup d'état and another government bent on surrendering to the Allies when things could very well be far from orderly; or else, and this seemed the most likely in view of the continued solidarity of purpose shown by the Germans, the battle would be fought until every square foot of territory had been occupied.

This would be the most dangerous as we would be inevitably caught up in the fighting, and we thought it prudent to prepare in favour of this eventuality. Accordingly we put our heads together and tried to work out our priorities. I set the pace.

'Having been a paratrooper,' I said, 'I feel we should see ourselves not merely as prisoners but as agents dropped behind the enemy lines for the particular purpose of finding everything out about Naunhof that may be of value to our side when they arrive. The collection of information I would see as our first task, coupled with the need to keep ourselves accurately informed about the daily situation on the fronts. How are we now off *vis-a-vis* the BBC?'

Jean replied. 'Soon after you left Alex managed to build a set into his guitar. Unfortunately the valves are now kaput and he has not been able to get any more.'

'That's a blow.'

'Attendez. Larry has been working on an old widow whose house lies behind the revier, separated by the length of our two gardens. He has been helping her cultivate her vegetables, the guards have raised no objection to that and she now turns a blind eye to him slipping in to her parlour and tuning in on her radio.'

'Is she reliable?'

'Larry thinks so. Absolutely. She told him her husband lost his leg in the last war and she has been against this one from the beginning. She says she is not afraid of the Nazis because she is an old woman and will not live much longer anyway.'

'Larry must risk making a regular arrangement with her. If he is unable to be there to get the news, she must. Do the guards suspect anything?'

'Not as far as I know. Glebens Leben still thinks he is winning the war and keeps them up to the mark with snap visits. I think they would report her to him if they found out.'

I pondered. 'We do not want to get the widow into trouble, but we have to have the news. Agreed?'

'Agreed.'

'Next we shall want the names of the key men in the town and where they live.'

'That will he the Burgomeister for one,' Jean started ticking off on his fingers, 'the führer of the local Volksturm for another, the men in charge of telephones, water, electricity, gas …'

'OK, that is a start. May we give that task to you and your fellows?'

'Bien sur.'

'I propose Alex and I try to get hold of a map of the town, and if we cannot we make one. And what about the population? We need to know

147

their attitude and where their real sympathies lay, whether they will fight or not when it comes to it.'

'That is true. I have heard it said that every able-bodied man and woman has been called-up into the Volksturm and issued with rifles.'

'All the more point in trying to find out if they mean to use them. It could make a big difference.'

We kicked about a few more ideas and then got down to briefing the various prisoners whom we thought might be instrumental in ferreting out the information we wanted. It gave us a great sense of purpose and a feeling of solidarity one with another, and was of untold value as a form of occupational therapy. This was something badly needed, as the next two or three weeks turned out to be a nail-biting period of waiting when nothing seemed to be happening, when the bridgehead at Remagen never seemed to get any larger.

During this time the routine followed the pattern of my previous residency; easily managed sick-parades and visits to Grimma. Whenever possible Alex and I took a walk in the town, covering all the roads, pacing out distances, noting this and that, anything we felt might be of use, the weather improving all the time and the hard winter very much a bad dream of the past.

Then suddenly everything changed. On 22 March the American 3rd Army got across the Rhine south-west of Frankfurt. On the 23rd British and Canadians made a full-scale crossing in the north. The next day Patton's army made another crossing south of Koblenz, and by the 27th the Allies had mastered the Rhine all the way from Nijmegen in the north to south of Koblenz. A finger growing daily into a bulge pointed towards Kassel in the centre and then became a breakthrough. For ten glorious days the ironclad legions of the Allies swept irresistibly in our direction. Kassel fell, one hundred miles to the west, halfway between Leipzig and the Rhine, and still the advance went on. It looked as though nothing could stop it. Our guards said. 'It is finished. It is only a matter of time.' The widow who had become our ally was jubilant, and the inhabitants of Naunhof looked at us somewhat differently. One said to me, 'you will not be a prisoner for very long now,' and smiled.

Only Oberstabsarzt Glebens Leben, still in charge of the military hospital in the town and of the revier, remained true to his previous form, strutting around in boots and spurs, continually complaining I was too lenient, always ready to fly into a rage. Once when I argued with him about a prisoner's fitness for work he flew off the handle, shouting.

'You say the British prisoners are sick when they are fit. So I will say they are fit when they are sick.'

I tried to remonstrate but he simply shouted me down.

'Please remember you are only a prisoner of war, and in no position to criticise a senior German officer.'

He then proceeded to suit his actions to his words and to mark as fit all those I had selected as unfit, telling them under no circumstances to report sick again for at least eight days. Why eight I never understood. There was no element of fear in his make-up. Perhaps it was due to lack of imagination. It never seemed to cross his mind the boot might soon be on the other foot. He was a convinced Nazi, or he posed as one, in whom faith in a Nazi victory was as yet unshaken. The newspapers and radio continued to blazon forth the confident belief that the Allies would be held. 'We must gain time,' they repeated again and again, 'for our new weapons to become effective. Defeat is unthinkable. Our Führer is invincible.'

'I suppose,' I said to Jean, 'he still thinks the British are military idiots.'

Jean was inclined to be pessimistic. The Allied advance had become slower and eventually come to a standstill east of Kassel, before Nordhausen, Erfurt and Weimar.

'The breakthrough has over-reached itself,' he said gloomily, 'perhaps the Germans have something up their sleeve after all.'

'No,' I said firmly, 'we are still making steady progress in the north and south.'

'But it is the centre that interests us is it not?'

He was not to be reassured. There was no gainsaying the lack of any further immediate progress on that front.

Glebens Leben became even more officious, and we waited anxiously for news of a renewal of the offensive. It came at the end of the first week in April. We thrilled to a report from the BBC brought to us by Larry. 'The battle for Leipzig has begun.' The German radio said nothing for several days and then started to admit the loss of several towns in the line of advance eastward: eighty miles away, seventy, sixty, fifty, forty. We followed breathlessly on our maps. The Americans were now so much nearer than the Russians, although a short time ago they had been about equidistant, we no longer countenanced the possibilty of the latter reaching us first. Had we then known it we need never have worried in any case, for the River Elbe had been agreed as a line of demarcation between the two groups upon which, at Torgau, later in the month they joined hands. The question now uppermost in our minds was not whether but how our liberation by the Americans would be effected. Would Naunhof be defended?

On 12 April prisoners coming in for a sick parade said rumours were rife in the town that American tanks had been sighted only twenty-five miles to the west, and that afternoon a large force of Lancaster bombers attacked railway targets between ourselves and Leipzig. Some of the prisoners working on the line had lucky escapes, and the planes passed very low overhead on their way back, to the consternation of many out on the streets who were seen scuttling to safety.

We had obtained the names and addresses we required, nearly all from the widow, now more and more openly on our side, and I had drawn a reasonable map of the town on the back of a temperature chart. We had also laid plans for an escape into the woods should the Germans attempt to force-march any occupants of the revier towards Bavaria whither, it was rumoured, many prisoner parties were already bound, and where Hitler was expected to make a stand if ejected from Berlin. In this event our widow had pledged herself to see we received food supplies and were kept abreast of the news.

Otherwise we decided our best battle strategy would be to secure ourselves in the cellars of the revier, and we laid in stocks of food and water. The German guards, as anxious on their own behalf as on ours, co-operated in this, looking more and more to myself for a lead.

The next day, the 13th, brought the first official signs the Americans were in the vicinity. The Burgomeister of Naunhof gave an order that all shops were to sell enough food to every citizen to last three weeks. This set off a general panic. The streets became full of women and children and old men all milling round the shops, filling baskets of every conceivable shape and size and the ubiquitous little hand-carts such as I had already remarked in Leipzig. There was a perpetual queue all day outside the baker's shop next to the revier, and prisoners mixed with it freely. From these contacts we learned that the mood of the citizens varied from resignation to keen anticipation of the arrival of the Americans, Most were looking forward to soon being out of the war and were as anxious as ourselves there should be no fighting in the town. The general consensus was that it would not be defended. At lunchtime the Americans were thought to be but fifteen miles away, and a proclamation came over the Leipzig radio instructing all unmarried women between the ages of eighteen and forty to report immediately to their nearest military headquarters for movement into the front line. This was followed by other instructions for the defence of the city. Later that afternoon I was informed by the Obergefreite that an order had come through from the Chefarzt at Oschatz that all sick in the revier able to walk were to be ready to march at dawn next day, and they were to be accompanied by the French doctor. I was to remain behind with the bed cases. Jean and I had been ready for this.

'Obergefreite,' I said, 'please tell the Chefarzt we have no patients in the revier able to walk. There will be none to accompany, therefore both doctors will be staying here.

The Obergefreite looked startled.

'Go on. At once.' I wanted to see how the Chefarzt would react. He received regular returns from all the reviers in the stalag informing him of the state of bed-occupancy and diseases under treatment, but without being on the spot he could not be right up to date. I guessed he would check it out with the Obergefreite upon whom I intended to lean as hard as I dared. But the Obergefreite changed the ball game and rang up Glebens Leben for confirmation of these instructions, and Glebens Leben ordered Jean to stay and myself to march. We now had received two totally different orders and could not comply with both, which gave us an opportunity for delaying tactics.

We intended to do our best to keep all the patients in the revier with one of us at least to look after them. If the Germans began to look trigger-happy, something that might occur in direct proportion to their nervous-ness, we agreed Jean would stay with the bed cases in the revier, while I, with the American captain, Alex and Larry, would take to the woods, with as many of the walking sick who wished to come; easier said than done as we realised only too well. It could involve an attempt to disarm the guards.

I again tackled the Obergefreite. 'We cannot accept the Oberstabsarzt's orders. They are in contradiction to those from the Chefarzt. I demand that you convey our previous reply to him, and report back what he says, to me, at once.'

'Certainly Herr Stabsarzt, right away.'

The Obergefreite was very anxious to please, to please both ourselves and his superiors. I felt for him but was obliged to put on the pressure. He made frantic phone calls but we were lucky. The Chefarzt was not immediately available, and it was not until late that night a reply was received from him to the effect his original order must be adhered to and, even if there were no patients fit to walk, the French doctor must himself be ready to leave at dawn. Jean thought the reason for this lay in his previous bad disciplinary record with the Germans.

'It is a reprisal. They do not wish me to be liberated.'

But an unbelievable, chance remark of one of the guards threw another, pantomime light on it.

'The Chefarzt is being generous. He assumes you would prefer to escape deeper into the Reich than fall into the hands of the enemies who have invaded your country.'

Topsy-turvy land indeed.

I said to Jean, 'we shall have to take the bull by the horns and discover where we really stand with the Orbergefreite. It is beginning to look like a case of us or them.'

Jean's expression was doubtful, 'can we not play for more time?'

'We have only until tomorrow morning.'

'Do what you think best.'

Neither the Obergefreite, Glebens Leben, nor the Chefarzt were going to stop the American 1st Army. I felt the odds against our captors had so much lengthened it was the moment, now or never, to call their bluff and put our highest card on the table.

'Obergefreite. Please understand. No prisoner is going to leave this revier. Any use of force on your part will be reported to the Allies. Do not doubt it. Your names are already in their possesssion. We have seen to that. If you wish to avoid serious trouble you will cooperate with us, now.'

'But Herr Stabsarzt what can we do? We have our orders.'

'In a few days at most, Obergefreite, possibly in a few hours you will be the prisoners. You would do better to obey me rather than the Chefarzt who is many miles from here and has no exact knowledge of our situation. This is what you can do. You can tell the Chefarzt his orders were countermanded by the Oberstabsarzt. You can tell Oberstabsarzt Glebens Leben that we refuse to move from here because we have had two different orders. It will not be your responsibility. If he wishes us to move he must come and move us himself. For your own sake, I advise you, do not attempt to use force.'

I held my breath. A German soldier is so disciplined the very idea of disobeying his own superiors is as unnatural as abstaining from food and drink. But I could sense his reluctance to antagonise me. We were all in a precarious position, they no less than ourselves, and time was the balancing factor needing to be weighed by both sides, and couldn't be with any accuracy.

At length he picked up the phone and called Glebens Leben. There was a good deal of shouting from the other end and the Obergefreite who was, after all, only a corporal, looked as miserable as any man I had seen for a long time. Nevertheless he stuck faithfully to the brief I had given him and the upshot was Glebens Leben merely ordered him to keep us under close watch the rest of the night, and he, Glebens Leben would come down to interview us in the morning. The Obergefreite mopped his brow with a handkerchief.

'Herr Stabsarzt,' he said, 'tomorrow it will be very unpleasant.'

'You may leave it to me,' I replied, 'the Americans may be here by then.'

That night I slept only in fits and starts, my nerves on edge, listening for the longed-for rumble of tanks. The noise of gunfire was quite distinct, the sky lit by flashes and there was no doubt about the proximity of the fighting. It was like being back in Arnhem waiting and hoping for relief. Towards dawn I dozed off and then was suddenly wide awake. The Background noise had changed. I was listening to the clip-clop of horses hooves, the rattle of harness and the creak of carts. Jean and I hastily put on our overcoats and went out onto the balcony of our room, there to gaze in a mixture of astonishment and unbelief at the sight before our eyes. It was a ragged army in weary retreat, like Napoleon from Moscow; a sorry procession of skeleton-thin horses dragging farm wagons of every description, all crammed with soldiery drunk with sleep, interspersed with battered trucks and, here and there, old cars bearing officers sprawling on the seats in utter fatigue. Men were staggering along the pavements on each side of the road, some pushing bicycles, grey with exhaustion. It was the very epitome of defeat, the myth of German invincibility dead before the eyes of anyone who beheld that shuffling, drooping, wordless column passing for the best part of two hours through the streets of Naunhof – and beyond.

My heart leapt. 'Jean,' I cried, they appear to be going through. Not stopping. Do you realise what it all means? The defences to our west have crumbled and they do not intend to defend Naunhof.'

'Mon Dieu. What a spectacle. I believe you are right. Let us send out for more news, from the other end of the town.'

I went downstairs to find the Obergefreite. 'It is very important,' I said to him sternly, 'that we should know the intentions of the German troops. You have seen them?'

Obergefreite nodded sadly.

'Please send one of the guards, on a bicycle. I must know if there are any of them still in the town. As quickly as possible.'

The Obergefreite was clearly demoralised. He didn't demur, and it was not very long before the guard was back again with confirmation of our hopes. The army that had passed through was to take up positions to the east, on the last river defence line before the Elbe. We had been virtually abandoned by the Wehrmacht, and could expect the American advance guard within twenty-four hours. It was also believed that American tanks had cut the Halle-Leipzig road. The BBC, on the other hand, put the Americans rather further away, and we learned that prisoners from neighbouring camps had been forced onto the roads and were being marched in the direction of Dresden. We were by no means quite out of the woods yet. Nevertheless I was sure in my own mind the situation had radically altered and now, at the most, there could only be a few rearguards between us and our liberators. Time was all we needed and must play for and gain.

At about 10 am Glebens Leben arrived at the revier and I braced myself for the confrontation. But there was no confrontation. The situation had indeed changed. He was a totally different man. With the passage of the troops he had seen the writing on the wall, and at last accepted the inevitable. He advanced slowly into the room, hands low in front of him crossing scissor-wise, deprecatingly, like the action of a referee signalling the end of play. It was a moment of truth. We three, Jean, the American captain and myself stood around three sides of the table, while he came to stand at the other. There was a long pause while he searched our faces, and then he suddenly dropped his eyes and cut his hand down to an open book that lay in front of him. He flicked over a few pages and said, in a voice subdued with emotion,

'Gentlemen. The leaves have turned. I have come here to ask you what you propose to do.'

Again there was a pause while we digested this information, and then I, having already previously assumed the mantle of spokesman, at a nod from the others, answered him carefully in English, which Jean with some prompting from me in French, translated equally carefully into German.

'First, Glebens Leben, we do not propose anything. We intend remaining, all of us, in this revier. It is preposterous to suggest unfit men should march along open roads, exposed to the dangers with which all roads will be beset by land and air forces. And as they will remain so will we. We wish to be repatriated as soon as possible. Again, to remain in the revier offers our best chance. Second, we demand that our German guards also remain here to protect us from possible irresponsible actions by fanatics. Third, we demand that the existing arrangements for medical supplies and food should continue, with the ration increased to the full scale field allowance of the German Army. Fourth, we wish to be kept fully informed of the military situation as it effects Naunhof.'

He was beginning to drum on the table with his fingers, and broke in to what I was saying with a flash of his old hauteur,

'Haben Sie etwas mehr zu verlangen?' Verlangen means to demand, and he emphasised the word as I turned to Jean,

'Translate what he says into English or French please.' I stared hard at Glebens Leben as he did so.

'Yes, I have. I demand you agree to these demands forthwith and unconditionally.'

I knew I might be pushing it a bit but it seemed vital at this juncture to assert complete authority, to give him no loop-hole.

I continued to stare at him uncompromisingly until at last he lowered his eyes back to the book, and once again flicked over the pages.

'I agree to what you have demanded,' he said with a slight shrug of the shoulders, 'except,' with a wry grimace, 'I think you are already better off for food here than is the German army.' I did not rise to that but kept trying to stare him out of countenance. He nodded his head, as if trying to convince himself of something. 'I will withdraw to my own hospital and leave the responsibility for the sick here entirely to you.'

'Oh no you don't you slippery devil' I thought, every faculty I possessed concentrated on trying to keep a complete grip on the situation.

'No,' I replied sharply. 'You are entirely responsible for the welfare of this revier until the Americans take us over. Any shortcomings of supplies or security will be laid at your door.'

He glowered at me but eventually submitted, still wriggling,

'If you say so. But as doctors we must protect the interests of our own patients. Please inform me if the Americans take the revier, and I will inform you if they take my hospital.'

'Not "if" major. When! It is all agreed?'

'Agreed.'

After he had gone we shook hands all round and imparted the glad tidings to the patients. The only danger now foreseeable was, still, of becoming involved in a battle for possession of the town if the Volksturm should put up any serious resistance. It was unlikely but possible, but we felt, in our cellar, we should be safe from anything except direct hits from artillery shells or aerial bombs and we were not in a locality, as far as we could see, of any tactical value to defenders.

The days were beautiful; warm spring sunshine, blossom appearing on the trees and daffodils in full bloom. The clear skies brought a full-scale invasion of our part of the world that afternoon by American fighter-bombers. They waltzed about the sky diving at targets unseen to us and the air became clamorous with the noise of machine guns, and rocket explosions mixed with ack-ack fire. The Luftwaffe, as usual these days, was conspicuous by its absence.

I had taken up station on the balcony outside our bedroom as a good vantage point from which to watch our southern sector, as well as to enjoy the sun. I had installed a chair there and a book, the Forsyte Saga by Galsworthy, purchased in Leipzig, and at one point was sitting reading it, my feet on the balcony railings, when three Typhoons, of which I had been vaguely aware as a growing noise in the distance, flew right overhead to about two thousand feet, peeled off, and dived at teriffic speed seemingly straight at me. I watched fascinated, transfixed as they roared nearer until, seeing bursts of flame beading the leading edges of their wings, my reflexes took over, and hurling myself out of the chair and backwards into the room I dived full-length under the table, pursued now by the lethal sound of spitting machine-guns. It was quickly over. They must have passed a bare fifty feet above the revier. The railway line was only a block away, and it transpired their target had been the station and its rolling stock which were badly shot up.

The platform on our side was crowded with would-be passengers and some were injured, but the only person killed was the station-master. He could be described as the only legitimate animate target in the station and the Typhoons had miraculously singled him out. Jean was quick to realise the propaganda value of this to us, and we hastened to exploit it as evidence of the uselessness of resistance to such accuracy and of the Americans' desire to spare those not in any kind of uniform. Official Nazi sources had been trying to instil a mood of desperate defiance in the civilian population by publishing false accounts of atrocities committed by the Americans in places they had occupied. The story of the station-master soon became news item number one in Naunhof. He was, so we were given to understand, in any case an unpopular figure, known to us and on our list as an uncompromising Nazi, and his demise in these dramatic circumstances may well have been advantageous.

The widow had torn up some of her dresses and linen to make me a Union Jack and this I now furled ready to break out on the revier flag-pole as soon as the town fell. The Typhoon attack had given us a feeling of being in the front line, and during the hours of daylight we kept a look-out posted on the roof. Firing in the near distance was music to the ears as constant evidence of the transformation in our fortunes, and we needed it – it was all so unbelievable. From having been buried far away in the middle of Germany, in the darkness and grimness of Hitler's Reich, with friendly help hundreds of miles away, we were now on the very edge of an ever-dwindling island of enemy territory. After having been exposed to all the brash confidence, ruthlessness and outward strength of the Nazi world that ruled my life when I was brought to Naunhof for the first time, it was now all melting away and breaking up before my very eyes. Then it had seemed the war would never end, as if I might never again be free and now freedom was, perhaps, only a matter of hours away. The pace of events in these last few days had so accelerated that we, from having been spectators away even from the touch-line, suddenly found ourselves right in the game, involved as players, and I think all the prisoners, especially the older, long-standing ones, felt great difficulty in acclimatising themselves to our new role. It was something they had dreamed about and hoped for for years. They were like poor men who had won a large football pool, acquired a fortune. For a little while they did not know what to make of it. It was all too good to be true.

We went to bed late that night, feeling rather let down, wondering if it would be on the morrow we would wake up to find ourselves free.

Nothing further had happened. True, we were more or less our own masters but marking time – waiting, waiting. Apart from one or two loud explosions the hours of darkness passed uneventfully and so, somewhat to our dismay, did the following day. The local news was vague, the BBC indefinite. Rumour had it tanks had already by-passed Naunhof to the south and were pushing towards Dresden and the Elbe. It had become uncannily quiet. Trains had stopped running and even that intermittent clatter was missing. It was Sunday and we might have been in Victorian England, only nobody went to church and I played endlessly at cribbage with the American captain. Jean wandered restlessly about the town visiting his compatriots in their various lagers, sniffing for news. Apart from the sick in the revier, medical work was at a standstill. According to the Obergefreite men falling ill on the working parties were being taken direct to the hospital to be seen by Glebens Leben. Jean came back at lunch time without having learned anything of significance. The whole of Naunhof was holding its breath. The town was like a ship becalmed in the doldrums waiting to see from which quarter the next wind would blow. Streets were deserted, everyone lying low in their dwellings. Our guards were fidgety, anxious, Jean said, to avoid capture; not because they feared reprisals – I had assured them I would favour them with good reports and my protection, such as it might be worth when the moment came – but because they were worried about their families and wanted to make their several ways home, he had the radio on practically all day. The Leipzig transmitter was broadcasting nothing except music interspersed with short news bulletins, just as in England during the first days of the war. The bulletins were repetitive and vague, but at least indicated the Germans were still in control there.

During the afternoon another rumour started to gain ground: the Americans were massing for an assault, holding their fire so as not to give their positions away. We must expect a heavy artillery attack and aerial bombardment at any time. I do not know where this rumour started, nor how it got into the revier and in among the patients, but I found myself being called up to the ward to reassure them.

They knew what our plan was in such an event; to evacuate everyone to the cellars and close all the window shutters. In the garden a deep slit trench had been dug at a vantage point, to be manned in rotation by the German guards in order to keep the road under observation. In short, we proposed to batten down hatches and ride out the storm with one look-out posted to keep an eye on the weather. I explained all this again, as patiently as I could, to the men in the bunks, knowing how vulnerable they must feel on the top floor, assuring them the moment any kind of bombardment started the plan would be put into effect, that it was

157

only a rumour anyway and Naunhof was of no particular importance. The Americans' interest was in the elimination of the remnants of the German army and, as we knew there was none of it here, there was no reason why the town should be attacked. So the day passed; an anticlimactic day, difficult to cope with mentally at this time when everyone in the revier was suffering from liberation fever.

Monday dawned, without any obvious change in the military situation. I was so tensed up, wondering how the dénouement would come, I had hardly slept. I was not the only one; the inhabitants of the town must have been agonising over their fate, the Burgomeister above all. He got wind of a mass-meeting called for ten o'clock in the Platz, and Jean made sure we were represented among the crowd. At the appointed time the Burgomeister appeared from within the Rathaus and stood at the top of the steps to address the population. He had, he said, been wrestling with the problem of where his true duty lay, with Naunhof or the rulers of the Reich, and he had, after much painful thought, come to the conclusion that his responsibility for his fellow-citizens lay the most heavily on his conscience. He said events had forced the unwelcome conviction upon him it was only a matter of time before the whole of Germany was occupied, and that nothing he or the inhabitants of Naunhof could do would alter this inevitable course of events. This being so to offer resistance to the Americans was useless. It would be better to live and assist in the reconstruction of the country than die in a senseless attempt to stop tanks with rifles, which was all they had. Naunhof was a town of old men, women and children, and he would rather run the risk of being shot as a traitor than have the destruction of the town and its people on his conscience. By surrendering the town they could save it and themselves. It was for him to make the decision, and he had made it. No resistance would be offered to the entry of American forces. The Volksturm would now hand in all its arms at the Rathaus and go home. A sentiment echoed with loud cheers.

Jean's plant, a French prisoner working in a dairy near the Platz, had immediately hastened to the revier to bring us the report of what had taken place, and we were mightily encouraged and cheered by the news. It was the best possible – no fighting for Naunhof. A small crowd shortly formed outside the revier, and the Obergefreite said they were anxious to know if there was anything they could do to help the prisoners. I was wondering if they were just hedging their bets or if I should go and say something gracious to them, when Glebens Leben put in one of his unheralded appearances. From the room where we had had so many encounters I observed him get slowly out of his car, glance briefly at the people by the gate, and walk thoughtfully up the path to our front door, now, in token of our emancipation, left permanently open during the daylight hours.

'I wonder what he's up to this time,' I said to Jean.

'We should be on our guard,' he replied, 'that Bosch will not be full of thoughts for our well-being, of that one can be sure.'

And we needed to be.

'Good morning gentlemen,' he announced himself brightly, 'I hope all goes well?'

'Translate please Jean.' I was not only not going to speak with him in his language but was desirous of the time the translating process would give me to think about what he was saying and how I might reply.

'I bring you good news. Naunhof is to be surrendered without a fight.' He paused to observe the effects of his words, not knowing we were ahead of him. I merely nodded.

'Please continue.'

'I am here to suggest it will be in the best interest of all if you, Herr Stabsarzt, take over my hospital, and also approach the Burgomeister with a request to take over the town. I am ready to surrender my hospital and he is ready to surrender Naunhof.'

I was astonished to say the least. 'I take over your hospital and the town?'

'Yes. That is what I have come to suggest.'

This was a turn in affairs I had never foreseen, and was something I clearly needed to consult Jean and the American captain about before giving him an answer.

'We must confer among ourselves major; please excuse us a moment.'

I led the others upstairs to the privacy of our room. 'Well what do we make of that? It's astounding. Do you think he's joking?'

'No,' said Jean, 'he cannot be joking. He has no sense of humour.'

The only combat soldier among us was the American captain, and he had only one eye and an unhealed socket where the other had been. How could one other doctor and one disabled soldier take over a town? But it was tempting. I turned to our American friend.

'It is your army in the offing. If we could do it we could hand Naunhof over to then on a ready-made plate. Do you think it's at all a practical proposition?'

'No way,' he said decisively, 'I guess the major's up to the old game of passing the buck. If the krauts could get you to take it on they would be able to shift the blame for anything that happened afterwards right onto your shoulders – and ours.'

Jean vigorously nodded his agreement, 'there could be food riots, private vendetta killings, anything, a mass exodus even.'

'Yeah, that's so, and we don't want the roads clogged with kraut refugees.'

'I take it then I turn it down.'

'Absolutement.'

'Yeah. Flat.'

Glebens Leben was pacing up and down the room we had left him in, with his hands clasped behind his back, and he looked up expectantly as we entered.

'Well, Gentlemen?'

'I thank you major for the suggestion,' there was no point in being brusque, 'but it would not be at all correct. The correct course to follow is for you to remain in command of your hospital, and the Burgomeister in command of the town until such time as the American forces arrive and take over.'

I hammered out the word 'correct' at him because I knew it counted for so much in the German mind. Then I had what I thought amounted to a real diplomatic brainwave.

'Furthermore,' I said, 'it would not be becoming to the dignity of the German people nor of the German army if their representatives, the Burgomeister and yourself, surrendered to a non-combatant. (There was irony in this I did not yet appreciate.) That is all, major, please convey my reply, and my respects, to the Burgomeister.'

Then, as he had so often with me, I allowed myself the pleasure of turning on my heel and leaving him in the room without a backward glance, to signify the interview was irretrievably concluded, and to rub in his own admission that the leaves had indeed turned.

The revier by now had become a focal point of civilian interest, and I found myself receiving deputations from members of the population wishing to declare their support for the prisoners, and their desire to help us in any way they could. I set up a 'command post' in the office and installed Alex as my deputy. He was so very well known in the town after all these years, and spoke such excellent German, I felt he would not only be able better to capitalise on such good will towards us as apparently existed, but would enjoy doing so. I only wished the American 1st Army would get on with it and put in as early an appearance as possible. I was neither an experienced campaigner, nor a trained diplomat, nor a born administrator. I was a relatively junior doctor with only two years behind me since qualification. I was, frankly, putting as mature and bold a face on things as I could, but inwardly feeling very unsure of myself and, like Glebens Leben, anxious to be relieved of my responsibilities.

Late that afternoon we received news, as reliable as any, there was fighting going on in a small village six miles away. I went up onto the roof to reconnoitre the position. Visibility did not extend that far and I could see nothing of the fighting, but I distincly heard the rattle of small arms fire. With the free contact we were now having with the people of Naunhof a stream of gratuitous information was coming in, and we were able to confirm that tanks had certainly by-passed the town to the south, and were beyond us advancing to the east. We reckoned we were in a pocket waiting to be mopped-up by the infantry, now probably engaged in this process in the village to our west. Knowledge about the tank movements was derived from a civilian, who told Alex he had been driving his car on an errand outside town and had suddenly been confronted by a mass of these ironclads advancing on a broad front at right angles to his route, his shock and surprise was such he had swerved off the road and only just stopped short of a ditch, very much afraid he might be about to become a target. Such is the perversity of human nature he was now feeling aggrieved because they totally ignored him, passing majestically across his front until, again alone, he had sheepishly reversed his car off the verge and returned post-haste to Naunhof.

The Burgomeister had ordered a strict curfew, and by sunset the bakery and precincts of the revier were deserted. Alex had earlier warned me the Obergefreite and guards were getting more and more restless, expressing a strong desire to shed their uniforms, don civilian clothes and try to rejoin their families. With nightfall I felt the time had come to lean heavily on the Obergefreite.

'You heard what Oberstabsarzt Glebens Leben agreed to?'

'Yes, Herr Stabsarzt.'

'You are to remain here to guard the revier until relieved by the Americans.'

'Yes, Herr Stabsarzt.'

'Those were the orders?'

'Yes, Herr Stabsarzt.'

'Then you will obey them?'

'Yes, Herr Stabsarzt.'

'Good. But do not be anxious, I will give you all an ausweiss as soon as they arrive – a pass that will be of greater value in getting you home than civilian clothes. Guard us and you will have earned a free passage.'

The Obergefreite bowed to the inevitable. I felt sorry for him.

'Where are your family?'

'Near Dresden.'

'Not too far away?'

'No. But nor are the Russians.'

'The Americans will get there first.'

'Do you think so?'

'Undoubtedly. You have a wife there?'
'Yes.'
'Anyone else?'
'Two children. Grandchildren.'
'Are they all well?'
'Yes, the last time I telephoned.'
'Have you telephoned recently?'
'No. The lines are cut.'
'They will be all right.'
'You think so?'
'The Allies do not make war on women and children.'
'Thank you, Herr Stabsarzt. These are terrible times.'

That night, soon after dark, we heard the noise of heavy-track vehicles passing along a road running in the direction of Leipzig to the north of Naunhof. Our American friend was sure they were tanks.

'That completes our isolation,' he said, 'we might as well go to bed and have a good night's sleep. The infantry will not contemplate any action until it is light. I'll bet any of you fifty bucks they'll be here sometime tomorrow.'

There were no takers.

Despite the optimistic tenor of our friend's prognosis I thought it prudent to maintain a shared watch during the night. I was mentally back at Arnhem, awaiting during the hours of darkness I knew not what, but certain we should be ready for anything. Two hours on duty for each of us. It was no great hardship. I said I would take the last trick, 4 am to 6 am, ready to receive the day whatever it had to bring. While the others were on watch I slept like a baby; so much water under the bridge, so many difficulties, so many dangers; I passed out into a haven of blessed oblivion until, reluctantly, I was shaken awake by Jean.

'All quiet on the western front. Nothing to report.'

That morning, the 17th, at about breakfast-time, a lone, unarmed Medical Orderly belonging to the 69th American Infantry Division, having lost his way, blundered into Naunhof in a Jeep and, finding himself in the Platz, stopped before the most imposing building there, the Rathaus, with the intention of trying to establish his whereabouts. There being nobody in sight in the square he advanced up the steps and agitated the knocker on the Rathaus door. It was opened by the janitor who, seeing the uniform, bolted back inside the building, and very soon returned with the Burgomeister. The Burgomeister identified himself and formally requested the Medical Orderly to accept his surrender. The Medical Orderly, being more concerned to rejoin his unit, replied brusquely.

'You'll have to wait, Buddy, I'm busy.'

The Burgomeister, not having achieved his position without some irate resourcefulness, replied to the effect that there were Allied medical officers in the town eagerly awaiting his arrival, and he would be very glad to escort him to them.

'You mean they've been expecting me?'

'For a long time. Please allow me to show you the way.'

'Well. OK.'

The Burgomeister climbed into the Jeep, and the next thing we knew of this in the revier was an unscripted burst of cheering from a group of citizens queuing at the bakery. I came to stand before the front door, flanked by Jean and the American captain, with Alex, Larry, the French orderlies, the Obergefreite and the guards drawn up behind. The occupants of the Jeep descended and approached up the path. At the threshold the Burgomeister halted before me, turned to indicate the now somewhat bemused American orderly, and announced in a grave voice,

'Our liberator is here.'

'Hiya!' said the liberator.

'OK,' said our American captain, stepping forward to shake his hand, 'good to see yer.'

And with that all protocol was abandoned.

The two Americans embraced each other. Jean embraced me. I shook hands with everybody in sight, and the lookers cheered like mad. After a little while a silence fell, and I was aware of people's eyes looking expectantly in my direction, something more was being called for – words of some kind to mark the occasion. I coughed nervously and looked at Alex. He nodded. 'Well then,' I said, 'will you translate whatever I say into German. Not too fast. Give me time to think.' I took a couple of paces forward to isolate myself, thinking like fury.

'All of us here ... have witnessed something this morning ... we shall remember the rest of our lives ... It is a great satisfaction to me ... that this town and this prisoner-of-war medical unit ... has been liberated by a member of the Allied medical services ... We stand for the relief of pain and suffering ... and I hope and believe after this war is finally ended ... the world will be guided by those same humanitarian principles ... that have always enlightened the best members of my profession ...'

'My God,' I thought, 'is that really me saying that? High time to stop.'

'... And now, Alex, the flag please.'

Alex came to attention and marched smartly to the pole, set in the garden on one side of the path, felt inside his battle-dress blouse and produced the widow's Union Jack. with great deliberation he attached it to the halyard and, as he bagan to raise it, I, sensing I had now become *de facto* officer-in-charge of the revier, looked round and gathered up in my glance the knot of poeple in the garden and the crowd outside and, in the parade-ground voice I had not used since leaving England, called everyone to attention. I held them there for a minute or two then, 'Stand at Ease ... Stand Easy.'

'Three cheers for His Majesty King George the Sixth, and the President of the United States! Hip Hip ... Hip Hip ... Hip Hip.'

It was an emotional moment.

What next? Our American officer friend suggested he should accompany the 'liberator', who was itching to return to his unit, a battalion which had spent the night a mile or two away, to contact the Commanding Officer, inform him of the situation here and bring back a more substantial force properly to occupy the town. Having seen him off I approached the Obergefreite and ordered him to hand over to me the keys of the 'armoury', a cupboard in his office where he and the guards kept their rifles. I issued one each to Alex and Larry and told them to take some of the sick prisoners with minor ailments out on a foraging party, warning them to carry the rifles slung, that they were only for protection and there was to be no show of force. I do not know by what devious means the foraging party tracked down its quarry but it returned loaded, with sides of bacon, sacks of chickens, bottles of brandy – and champagne.

The celebration that ensued was noisy and rumbustious. We ate and drank far too much, the drink going straight to our heads, and in the middle of it all I suddenly remembered the Obergefreite and the guards.

'We should share some of the fruits of liberation with them Alex, do go and ask them to join us.'

'Good idea, shir. Won't be a dshiffy.'

Jiffy was the right word for it he was back in no time, breathless from running up the stairs.

'They've gone. shcarpad. No shign of them anywhere.'

'You shore?'

'Absholutely.'

I put down my glass, suddenly sobered, and just as well. For, as I rather carefully descended the stairs to look for myself our American friend walked in the front door accompanied by a figure in the uniform of an American major. I say 'figure' because he was wearing dark glasses and full combat equipment, and all I was conscious of at first were the pistols on his hips, grenades suspended round his waist, automatic weapon tucked under his left arm, battle-helmet clamped on his head, dusty uniform, trousers tucked into high-ankled rubber-treaded boots and a lean, tanned hand extending toward me.

'Good to see yer Doc.'

'And you, Major.'

'I've dropped a task force off down town. I'm told you know it pretty well.Would you care to drive round with me and show me my way about?'

'Gladly. I'll get my beret.'

I never went out without it as, being the only one in the area, it was my personal mark of identification. I also fetched the map I had made. If ever there was a victory parade, as far as I was concerned this was it; and the high-light was a visit to Glebens Leben in his hospital where his utter demoralisation was finally accomplished. I had briefed the major on our assessment of him as a convinced Nazi, and as one of the trickier customers around Naunhof. He had smiled grimly, 'leave him to me'. We picked up another jeep-load of his men, and as we drew up outside the hospital door they piled out, taking up watchful stations on either side. The major banged the knocker, pulled the iron ring of the outside bell and stood back, his automatic weapon at the ready. As soon as the door started to open he gave it a vigorous kick, and rushed in accompanied by two of his soldiers. I followed. We were in a cool, tile-floored hall, with the medical orderly who had been opening the door cowering by it with frightened eyes. At a signal from the major I spoke to him.

'The American major wishes to see the Oberstabsarzt immediately. Get him, schnell.'

I enjoyed saying 'schnell'. At another nod from the major a soldier detached himself from our group and, prodding the orderly with his gun, disappeared with him toward the back of the hall. When Glebens Leben appeared, covered by the soldier's gun, his normally sallow complexion was suffused with blood, and he looked extremely angry. But not for long. The major had asked me to act as interpreter and it gave me an unholy joy.

'Stand to attention please.' The major's automatic was pointing uncompromisingly at Glebens Leben's head, and the colour drained from his face.

'Have you a weapon?'

'No.'

'No – sir.'

'No – sir.'

'You lie.'

'No, sir.'

'What is that then?' he indicated a ceremonial dagger, with which German officers like to accoutre themselves, dangling from his belt. 'Hand it over immediately.'

'But ...' Glebens Leben would not like this; it was like surrendering a sword, equivalent to stripping him of his honour, his status.

'Immediately.'

I translated 'sofort', and added my now favourite word, 'schnell', for good measure.

Glebens Leben wearily unbuckled the dagger and morosely handed it over, his posture now drooping into a slouch.

'Stand to attention please.' He knew enough not to need my translation of this command. The major had barked at him, jolting him upright. I translated all the same.

'Listen very carefully,' the major's voice was very cold and menacing. I shall return in twenty-four hours and this hospital will undergo a thorough search. If any arms are dicovered you will be shot. You will not leave the premises without permission. If you do you will inevitably be found – and shot. That is all. You may dismiss.'

Glebens Leben threw me a despairing glance but I ignored it. He had had it coming to him.

The following day all the best houses of Naunhof were requisitioned as billets for the 69th Infantry Division, which set up its headquarters in the town. The Senior Divisional Medical Officer, a relaxed, humorous, very pleasant man, who carried a walking stick and moved unhurriedly about his business, visited the revier and discussed arrangements for our repatriation. The British would be passed down the normal medical lines of evacuation and flown home, the French, he thought, would be returned to France in empty supply lorries. These lorries, bringing stores to the front, were soon roaring through Naunhof all day as, in a very short time, we had become no longer a part of the front line but a back area, with hundreds of lines of communication troops swarming over the streets.

Jean said he would like to express his own thanks to our liberators by giving them dinner at the revier. He would guarantee a meal up to the best standards of French *haute cuisine*. If the Divisional Medical Officer and Divisional Commander would honour us with their presence it would give him great pleasure – but perhaps they would be so kind as to bring some glasses with them as we had none to drink out of.

The dinner was a great success. Jean's people did something stunning with chicken and, as our guests arrived bearing gifts of cigars, wine and more brandy we did ourselves proud. Too proud. Our stomachs were not used to it. I felt very ill next day, fortuitously as it turned out. For in order to accelerate our movement home we British were to be labelled as suffering from some ailment or other, and gastroenteritis could be inscribed on mine and tied to my person without simulation.

Within forty-eight hours of the arrival of the medical orderly in the jeep I was supervising the loading of our sick into a fleet of four-patient ambulances. Alex, for reasons only known to himself but I suspected an affair of the heart, said he wanted to remain at the revier for a bit, with Larry, and they would take their chance later. The Divisional Medical Officer arrived to see us off, bound for the nearest airfield, and it was with a lump in my throat that I said my good-byes. Jean and his compatriots would be staying on at the revier, using it as a collecting post, gradually mustering the very numerous French prisoners in the Naunhof area to take their turn for transportation to France.

We set off in a convoy for the airfield. My mind boggled. This was history repeating itself. I was mentally back with the 11th Parachute Battalion winding its way through the by-roads of Lincolnshire for take-off for Arnhem. That had been on 18 September 1944. Today was 19 April 1945 – not a long interval by many prisoner-of-war standards; but how is length of time to be measured? By the clock? Or by what has gone into the hours?

At the airfield we were shepherded into the Medical Inspection Room, where the labels with our diagnoses were tied to our left breast pocket button-holes with pieces of string. Then we had DDT powder puffed on our heads, inside our shirts and down our trousers. We hung about for the rest of the day waiting for air-transport, and eventually had to spend the night in makeshift quarters near the field. The Americans were extraordinarily solicitous for our welfare. They could not do enough. I still was not feeling too well and was, regretfully, unable to take advantage of the marvellous meals I was offered. But I did taste the bread, so white and light after the heavy black stuff I had been living on it was like eating angel cake.

I felt no impatience at the delay. In truth I sensed a reluctance in myself to abandon the life and circumstances I had come to know and live with for the now-difficult-to-imagine scene at home. That I wanted to get out of Germany I was in no fundamental doubt but, having been so long cut off and having made my life there, I was apprehensive of change. Lying on the grass in the warm sun on 21 April – birthday of Princess Elizabeth – on the perimeter of the airfield, and watching the comings and goings of C 47s, Dakotas like those that had borne me into battle, I felt in half a mind to ask to be transferred northwards to where the British were fanning out over the Hanoverian plain denied to them at Arnhem. Paratroopers had gone in again at the Rhine crossing. I felt a nostalgia for my old unit, for Colonel Lea, the CO, for Lonsdale, the second-in-conmand, for Dwyer my medical sergeant, and Adams my batman. What had become of them all? It was the Dakotas that did it, unleashing memories fit to unman me. Then I looked round at the sick from the revier, nearly all drawing contentedly on Chesterfields or Camels. There was a job to be finished. I would see them home. At length, two Dakotas taxied round to where we were gathered and came to rest, their engines idling, opposite our group.

'This is it fellers. Your turn. England, home and Beauty.' The despatcher, I supposed he was a despatcher, it was the only name I knew for the crewman who looked after human cargo in these machines, sauntered over to where we were and, with a smile as wide as General Eisenhower's, took an elbow here and a shoulder there and gathered us winningly into the body of the Dakota.

How the memories crowded in. The same smell, the same accommodation, the same quickening of the pulse. I sat myself down in the same place, one seat next to the door, back to the fuselage, where I had been positioned when last emplaned, sandwiched between my commanding officer and Fat Crawford, an old school chum responsible for intelligence. Then all the occupants had been in rude health, armed to the teeth, fighting fit, aggressive and cock-sure. Now we were a sorry lot physically, wan, drawn, suffering from the long deprivations of imprisonment, and the excesses of the last few days. And mentally? The Dakotas taxied for the take-off, ran their engines against their brakes, then followed each other down the runway; rumbling, shuddering, accelerating until, at last, they came free of the ground, smoothly climbing, fields and trees streaming past below.

'My God,' I thought, 'what happens if the engines fail? I haven't got a parachute.'